REAL WOMEN
DO IT
STANDING UP

REAL WOMEN DO IT STANDING UP

Stories from the Career of a Very Funny Lady

Leighann Lord

Virtual Fist Bumps
to some of the Funny Women
Who Have Inspired Me

Dr. Bertice Berry

Carol Burnett

Elayne Boosler

Rita Rudner

Marsha Warfield

Sister Phyllis (Sophomore year Social Studies teacher)

My Mom

LEIGHANN LORD

CONTENTS

AUTHOR'S NOTE

On my 20th anniversary in comedy, I posted this on Facebook:

Today – not all that long ago – I stepped on stage to do stand-up comedy for the first time and my life was forever changed. With a microphone in my hand I have traveled further, flown higher, and burned brighter than with anything else I could have chosen to do with my life. Stand-up has given me my deepest heartaches and my greatest joys. It has wounded and healed me. Stand-up comedy has introduced me to the most awesomely talented and deeply troubled people I have ever met; many of whom I am proud to call my friends and fans. I've given up many things to do stand-up and it has given me gifts beyond measure. Knowing what I know now, would I choose to do it again? How could I not?

That said, why didn't anyone stop me?

ONE MORE THING

Some of these stories were written when I had both a husband and a dog. I now have neither. I had to make the difficult decision to either exclude these pieces or update them. I chose to leave them intact not out of laziness but to preserve these experiences as they happened. They are painful but necessary reminders that life changes in ways that we can never imagine and we must cherish what we have when we have it; and also that I should publish faster.

IN THE CLUB

I used to have a corporate job. I had to give it up when I learned I'm allergic to the material they make cubicles out of: cardboard and bullshit.

ESCAPING THE CORPORATE CUBICLE

I left Corporate America to become a stand-up comedian. I'd only taken a day job because I thought I was supposed to. I graduated from college when then country was nipple-deep in an economic recession. Friends who had graduated the year before me with degrees in marketing and finance were scrounging to get jobs at Macy's and McDonalds. How could I, with a degree in journalism and creative writing, expect to do any better? Well, the prevailing wisdom at the time was that it was better to hire liberal arts majors – kids who had been taught to think – than business school grads who had been programmed. And so, the kid who really wanted to write and act took a job in the Corporate Communications Department at Chemical Bank as the Assistant Editor of Employee Communications. And they were going to pay me the astonishing sum of $25,000 a year plus benefits. How could I say no?

I started work on a Monday and by Tuesday I knew I'd made a horrible mistake. But I didn't know how to change it. I felt stuck. How could I tell my parents I was quitting a job paying real money to be a performing artist? I'd had a hard enough time telling them I'd changed my major. (Actually, I still haven't told them so let's keep that between us, shall we?) That sort of carrying on was fine when I was in school but I was in the real world now. They'd be expecting a return on their substantial investment. I'd watched them go to jobs every day they hated and now it was my turn, right?

In retrospect it was a good job with a solid company. And for the most part I worked with nice people. And yet the five years I spent there are still the sickest I've ever been in my adult life. I had headaches, frequent colds, and chronic fatigue. When my boyfriend would drop me off at the subway in the morning, I'd sit in the car crying and say, "Please don't make me go." We'd drive away and I'd call in sick, again. And when I wasn't absent, I was late. I used up most of my vacation days as sick days. And if this illness had a name it was despair. Because everything about this job felt wrong, like I wasn't supposed to be there and I was miserable. I felt like I was dying on the inside.

It took me three years to realize that no one was going to rescue me from my cubicle. If I wanted out, I'd I have to do it myself.

My journey out started with a simple question: If I'm not happy how do I get there from here? I remembered that I'd always been happiest when I'd been writing, performing, and making my friends laugh but I didn't know exactly what to do with that. I still wanted to act, but it was clear at the time that non-traditional casting was a college thing and no one was tripping over themselves to cast a journalism graduate with a minor in theatre from a business school.

In the midst of all this soul searching, my boyfriend got us tickets to a live TV taping of this hot new HBO comedy show called *Russell Simmons' Def Comedy Jam*. I remember sitting in the balcony and watching comedian Michael Collier tell a Rodney King joke. He said, and I'm paraphrasing:

"I turned on the TV and saw Rodney King getting his ass beat, and I got mad. I called my agent and said, 'How come I didn't get to audition for that Timex commercial?'"

The audience was completely silent for a moment as we made the connection with Timex's slogan: "Takes a licking and keeps on ticking." When we did, the power and force of our response ripped through the theatre like a tidal wave. I can still feel it.

What was truly magical for me was watching Michael wait. He put the joke out there and waited for the audience to get it. He was patient and confident. And when we got it, he absorbed the roar of our appreciation with a calm and cool majesty. And I thought, "I. Want. To. Do. That."

After that, I loved my day job. Instead of being a trap that was sucking the life out of me, it was the good fortune that was going to finance my dream. The real test though was telling my parents. I was convinced that comedy was what I wanted to do with my life and their opinion didn't matter. But it did.

I told my Dad first because he's always been the more reasonable one. (My Mom is a "beat-first, ask questions later" kind of mother.) I said, "Daddy," (you know it's big when I say Daddy instead of Dad). I said, "Daddy, I've given this a lot of thought and I want to go into comedy. I want to be a stand-up comedian." My Dad smiled and said, "What took you so long?"

It's one thing to have people in your corner but to have them in your corner, waiting for you to show up? Well, it doesn't any get better than that, my friends.

A few years later my Parents were in the audience, sitting in the balcony, when I taped *Def Comedy All-Star Jam*.

Believe it or not, when I was invited to audition for the show I was reluctant. I was not then, nor am I now, a *Def Jam*-style comic. I'm not urban. I'm urbane. But it was an opportunity and so when they selected me to do the show I just tried to be myself. And according to the fan emails I've received over the years, it worked. The one that still touches me the most is this one:

"Leighann, My name is Lakeenya, and I just recently watched you perform on Def Comedy Jam. I think you bring a sense of intelligence and sophistication to the stage. Most audiences expect the demeaning and (profane) language that is easy to acquire in one's material. Which is why you surpass all others. Not only do you not lower your pride or intellect by taking the lazy and easy way, you also leave the audience with something to think about. You provide the world with an overview of a strong intelligent black woman. The ironic thing is, after watching you and the others, not only could I not remember what the other acts were about, I could recite yours line by line. That's when you know that you have seen a really great performance."

If I had stayed in that cubicle I never would've gotten that email. I remain humbled and awed by it. It reminds me that we each have a responsibility to find and pursue our passion. Finding your passion is the gift you give to yourself. Pursuing your passion is the gift you give to other people. Learning how your passion affects them is the gift that re-inspires you – usually when you need it most – to take a licking and keep on ticking.

That is the creative circle of life.

AUDIENCE MEMBER
Aren't you afraid to get on stage?

ME
No. I'm afraid not to.

My First Time

It was a Tuesday night at the World Famous Comic Strip in New York City: I thought I was ready. But the closer I got to my stand-up comedy debut, the more terror settled in. I heard that not-so-little voice mocking me: "You're not funny. They're not gonna laugh at you. You're gonna be humiliated in front of your friends."

I didn't really care about the full room of strangers at the club. I'd never see those 68 people again. But if I bombed in front of people who knew me how could I show my face again? I'd have to move, change my phone number, and get some new friends. None of which was in the budget.

I wasn't ready to be totally public. I only invited two of my closest friends to watch me potentially make a fool of myself. I knew one friend would be brutally honest about my performance; the other would have the decency to lie to me even if I was horrible.

I wasn't the only first-time comic on the show. There were four of us, mixed in with the professionals, who had taken a stand-up comedy class taught by the emcee. This performance was our "graduation," or more correctly, our baptism by fire.

Then it happened. The emcee introduced me: "Leighann Ford, ladies and gentlemen! Leighann Ford!" That voice inside my head tried to convince me that I couldn't possibly be the next comic. My last name is Lord, not Ford. But unlike David Berkowitz I ignored the voice, and went out on-stage.

Standing there, lights in my face, microphone in hand, strangers staring at me expectantly, the fear abated — just a little — to make room for another feeling: exhilaration. I told my first joke and the audience laughed. I wasn't prepared for that.

I'd envisioned an assortment of produce being thrown; outraged citizens storming the stage clamoring for my arrest, angry that I'd wasted their time and money; my mother weeping. But people other than my friends actually smiling and laughing? The pleasant surprise of it made me forget my next joke. In retrospect that was probably for the best, but that was okay. I felt like I had finally found where I was supposed to be. I felt at home. I was hooked! And best of all, according to both my friends, I didn't suck!

I've performed thousands of times since then, but sometimes I'm surprised by how little has changed. Emcees still mispronounce my name. I still get a tiny twinge of fear just before I go on. I still love the rush I get when the audience laughs at my opening joke, and when they do, I get hooked again, just like the first time.

"Baby, you love me because my birthday is on the second and your birthday is on the fourth. Now two is a factor of four, four is a multiple of two; two squared is four and the square root of four is two. The sum total of this means that your love for me is a factor, a multiple, a power, and a root of a love that was meant to be and therefore can exist in any quadrant on the X, Y, or Z-axis. You see Baby, numbers don't lie: you love me."

The Geometry of Love & Comedy

After a college show, a student came up and said, "Thanks for the 'D' student joke. I'm mentoring a high school student this weekend and you explained better than I could why he should get good grades." My joke:

"The most important thing I've learned watching TV crime shows is that it pays to be an 'A' student. If you're an 'A' student and you go missing, they look for you. If you're a 'D' student, you'll be duct taped in the trunk of a car thinking, 'Wow, I should have studied more.'"

That joke has come a long way. When I first began doing it, it got nothing, not even polite laughter. I was disappointed because I believed the premise to be both true and funny. I persisted. I tweaked the wording and placement, and eventually started getting a positive response. The joke didn't kill but it finally did well enough for me to get out of my own head (over thinking the wording and construction) and really focus on the audience. I noticed there was no middle ground. The people who liked the joke loved it and those who didn't were downright frosty.

One night, I addressed this schism from the stage. I said something like, "Ah, I see who the 'A' students are. 'D' students? Glad to see you made it out of the trunk, clearly all on your own. Congratulations." That did it. I won over the non-laughers, not completely, but there was a definite a thaw. I felt foolish for not realizing sooner that the people most likely to enjoy this joke had indeed been 'A' students.

For the others I'd probably touched on their not-so-subconscious fear that a less than stellar academic performance would earn them neither a scholarship nor a search party. In the event of their possible demise precious police resources would not be expended on them at least not to the degree that we've come to love on TV crime shows like *Law & Order* and *CSI*.

In that light, my joke seems to smack of academic elitism. That's a dangerous thing to do in the Decade of the Dumb Ass, but I'll risk it.

It's not all on the audience though. It's inevitable that when you do a new joke and it doesn't get the gut-busting reaction you hoped it would, you lose a little faith in it. You have to make a decision: fix it, shelve it, or dump it. When I understood how the audience perceived the joke I remembered my comedy mentor saying, "Tell a joke 100% or don't tell it at all." Lack of commitment in delivery and demeanor will sabotage a joke every time. When I told the joke without apology it went from being on the verge of getting dumped to being applauded. Sweet.

Now, it doesn't always work out that way. Sometimes a joke is just not funny or at least not funny for every audience. In those moments you're left standing on stage with just the fig leaf of your confidence. It's better than nothing, but not by much.

So, it was particularly rewarding when the college student mentor and his high school mentee not only complimented me on my joke, but also cited it as being helpful. As if to assure us that he was doing well in school and not destined for an extended stay in the trunk of a car, the high schooler spoke up and said, "But I am an 'A' student."

"Then tell him he needs to study for his geometry test on Monday," his mentor shot back.

It would have been so cool if I'd had some jokes about geometry right then, but alas no. So I said, "You should study for your geometry test. But honestly, in 10 years, you won't need it ... unless you want to play pool." I had his attention. "Playing pool is all about angles. That's geometry. And taking a girl out to play pool can be a fun first date. But hey, it's up to you." Of course we all know that if he really wants to be good at pool he'll need some physics to go along with that geometry but that's a lesson for another comedy show. The high school kid was speechless. His mentor looked at me appreciatively and again said, "Thank you."

"No," I said. "Thank you."

I used to feel bad for smokers, having to go outside and smoke in the cold, but then I realized if they're willing to risk cancer, pneumonia ain't no biggie.

SMOKING ALLOWED

It was a happy day for me when smoking was banned in bars and clubs around the country. I don't miss standing on stage and being enveloped by the slow moving but relentless blue haze that seemed to creep straight out a Stephen King novel. I've gotten use to breathing deeply at bars and only smelling disinfectant and desperation. That changed when I did a show at Karma Lounge in New York City.

A small sign above the door said *Smoking Allowed* but my brain dismissed it thinking it must be one of those quaint holdovers from back in the day. Mere decoration, I thought. So when I walked in it took my nose a few minutes to identify what was happening. *Wait ... that's not ... but ... oh ... the sign was right?* I was not happy.

I later learned that smoking is allowed at Karma because it's a Hookah Bar. As my eyes adjusted to the dimness it was a throwback to see smokers at their leisure. They were standing up right, relaxed, and content. I've become so accustomed to seeing them furtively smoking outside in hunched, harried, and huddled groups that this new posture looked almost brazen. I felt happy and sorry for them at the same time. Modern convention has turned them into the Untouchables, and not the sexy crime-fighting kind.

My sympathy however was short-lived as the carcinogenic cloud attached itself to me like a cat that heads for the person in the room who is most allergic to it. I'd like to say my tolerance for the smell of smoke isn't what it used to be, but it wasn't all that strong to begin with. When smoking in nightclubs was a ubiquitous fact of life I had a handbag full of defenses. When someone next to me lit up a cigarette, I would light up a stick of incense. If they protested I'd say, "You smoke what you want and I'll smoke what I want."

I also carried scented candles. The bartender at the now defunct Pips Comedy Club would always ask me for the one that smelled like maple syrup. As the comfort food-aroma battled with burnt tar he'd smile and say, "Now I'm in the mood for pancakes."

It's been a long time since I've needed to have those tools at the ready. So, I walked into Karma unprepared. But the longer I stayed – the things I do for stage time – the more my senses eventually adjusted to the smoky environment. I had almost convinced myself that the smell wasn't that bad. And it wasn't until I left the club.

The fresh night air hit me and stirred up the smoky scent that had laid itself on me like a layer of radioactive dust. I had an "Oh dear god is that me?" moment. The one you usually have late in the afternoon when you realize that you forgot to put on deodorant. The smoke had worked its way into my skin, clothes, and hair. I smelled horrible. I couldn't stand myself.

I knew that I'd be up very late doing laundry, showering, and washing my hair. Sure I could let the clothes wait, but there was no way I could put ass to mattress or head to pillow smelling like an ashtray. I also couldn't go to bed with a wet head of hair.

It was going to be a long night but I thought I'd at least have the company of my insomniac Cocker Spaniel. But when I got home he sniffed me, sneezed, and took his leave. He stomped off to the bedroom, curled up on his pillow, and was snoring within minutes; so much for unconditional dog love. Either second-hand smoke makes my Dog sleepy or he's a militant anti-smoker who's not above using the tool of social ostracism to make his point. If the latter, I'm lucky he didn't also bite me before turning his furry back on me.

It's one thing to be stink-eye snubbed by strangers. But to be shunned by a loved one, by a being you feed, house, and care for ... I suddenly knew how the parents of teenagers must feel. I think I also know how smokers feel. You smell bad and nobody likes you. You need a place of refuge. That place is Europe. But if that's not in the budget, I know a place where you might find some good Karma.

My *Vagina Monologues* Playbill Interview

QUESTION

What's your Vagina's (nick) name?

ME

Her Ladyship.

QUESTION

If your Vagina could get dressed, what would it wear?

ME

An invisibility cloak.

QUESTION

If your Vagina were a piece of furniture or home decor,
what would it be?

ME

I don't know. I'm still looking around for the perfect piece.

QUESTION

What's your Vagina's current mood?

ME

Persnickety.

QUESTION

What's your Vagina's motto or slogan?

ME

Remember where you are. This is *Thunderdome*. Death is
listening. And will take the first man who screams.

I HAVE A TATTOO ON MY VAGINA, WANNA SEE?

Saturday Night, First Show: Beverages in hand, smiles on their faces, the audience members are happily chatting with each other. They're out having a good time and they know it's about to get better. House lights go down, stage lights come up, and the hum of conversation is replaced by enthusiastic clapping as the emcee takes the stage. It's show time. Let the laughs begin.

And then there's Saturday Night, Second Show.

Saturday Night, Second Show at a comedy club can be a bit of a free for all. It's not as raucous as the now almost extinct third show, but for a low-energy, highbrow, monologist it can easily rank right above a root canal. At a recent Saturday Night, Second Show, the audience was dominated by a large group of young'uns celebrating a friend's 21st birthday.

Age is not necessarily an accurate predictor of how an audience will or will not behave. Any comic who's played a senior citizen center will attest that old folks can get rowdy too. Any big monolithic group mixed in with a general audience can be high maintenance. Sometimes any attention you pay the former only fuels their desire for more. While it would be kind to say that this particular group of young people was high-spirited, the truth is they were loud, obnoxious, and disruptive.

The young women in the group were screamers. Anything the MC said to or about them elicited a loud and prolonged "Wooooooooo!" the young-girl call of the wild usually only heard during spring break. Comedy icon Larry Miller once said to me that he didn't like the screaming. "If they're screaming, they're not listening."

By contrast, the young men in the group started out sullen and silent. They were simply biding their time, waiting for the alcohol to give them the courage to demonstrate how much funnier they were than the professionals on-stage. As the evening wore on, the liquor obliged.

Whose responsibility is it to deal with a rowdy crowd? Some comedians relish the opportunity. I do not. I do comedy, not combat. I think a venue's obligation extends beyond merely seating and serving. Ideally, you shouldn't have to tell adults how to behave, but when management does nothing it is abdicating its responsibility to the well-behaved patrons who have also paid to see a show.

Glancing around the audience I saw quite a few people who were visibly annoyed that these *Jersey Shore* hopefuls were being allowed to dominate so much of the show. Unfortunately, the fact that they were seated front and center of the stage made it impossible for me or the other comics to ignore them, as would have been my preference.

Post show, I was sitting at the bar mulling over career paths not taken when a woman from the offending group staggered over and proceeded to tell me how great she thought I was. She couldn't have been referring to my stand-up. I hadn't done any. Her compliment must have been for my verbal jousting skills, my ability to shovel impromptu witticisms against the imbecilic tide.

She apologized for the behavior of her group but

confessed that she really didn't know them. They were friends of her boyfriend and they were "young and immature." Indeed. This is the same woman who inexplicably shouted out in the middle of my show, "Let's talk about sports."

"Hmm, let's not."

Since we were now "friends" she offered to show me her tattoos. "I have a Yankee tattoo on my vagina! Wanna see?"

Offers like these are why some guys become comedians. They live for these chance meetings with The Drunk Girl at the bar, willing to over-share. "Uh ... no," I said.

But she really wanted to show me. And what drunken people want, drunken people get. She lifted up the front of her shirt, unbuttoned the top of her jeans, and showed me a tattoo that was, thankfully, just a modest two inches south of her belly button. I have nothing against alcohol, just the people who can't hold it. After what felt like decades, Tattoo Girl wandered off to flash someone else.

I sat a while longer at the bar, sipping my coffee, and decided in the end not to quit comedy just yet. Saturday Night, Second Show is just one of the hazards of the trade.

It's getting a lot harder to tell if someone is just rude, home schooled, or mentally ill.

THAT GUY

Every now and then I meet That Guy, the one who always wanted to be a comedian. That Guy is very funny around his friends and they tell him he should be on-stage. His friends are wrong. But at their urging, That Guy has done stand-up a few times — a few open mics here and there — but he didn't really have the time to pursue it seriously. But to hear That Guy tell it, if he had he'd certainly have his own TV series by now.

But in lieu of that, That Guy books and hosts his own comedy show because hanging out with the pros lets him pretend that he's one too. Around other comics he is – as we say in trade – "always on." He doesn't engage in actual conversation. It's all constant trash talk and verbal roughhousing because that's how comedians speak with each other right? That Guy loves giving jokes to comedians that he says would be perfect for their acts, and they would be if the jokes didn't already belong to someone else.

So I shouldn't have been the least bit surprised when That Guy — the emcee that night — went on-stage and said, "Let's have another round of applause for Leighann Lord. You can find her on Playboy.com where you can see pictures of her ass."

Did That Guy think he was being funny? Sadly, yes, but as a rule: if no one else is laughing, then it's not funny. It didn't help that he continued to make comments off-stage about how it was difficult for him to concentrate on the show because he was looking at my ass. Wow, how smooth was that?

I know I can't control what people think, but if it were okay to blurt out everything that's on your mind, Turrets Syndrome wouldn't be considered a neurological disorder. I carry myself as a lady and expect to be treated as such; hence the name of the actual website where you can find me: VeryFunnyLady.com, sans pictures of my posterior, of course.

I wish I could say that I confronted That Guy, he saw the error of his ways, and he apologized. I did confront him and my reward was having my future dates at the club cancelled. A small price to pay for my dignity, I suppose. But in the end, pun intended, I'd rather have a nice ass than be one.

Fantasy Job Posting on Monster.com:

Troubled world religion seeks new leader.
Must look good in tall hats and red shoes.
Fluent Latin a plus.

For the Love of Strangers

The comedy club was packed — standing room only. The line to get in was out the door and growing. Some folks tried to cut line and a fight broke out. Thankfully, Security squashed it quickly and no one was hurt. And I thought "Wow, y'all. It's just jokes." As the room surged past capacity the audience of strangers pulled it together. As if to erase the memory of the front-door fisticuffs they scrunched up, shared what few seats were left, and some folks were even sitting on the floor. I was performing at The Punchliner Comedy Club on a cruise ship, the Carnival Destiny. The audience had already seen me the night before last and had come back for more. Woo Hoo!

Uh oh.

One of the stand-up comedy facts of life is that it doesn't matter how funny you were last night, you better bring it tonight; right now. Just like in finance, past performance is no guarantee of future funny but the full house in front of me believed otherwise.

I stood in the back of the room taking it all in. Before a show, most people assume that I want to be alone in the green room (or whatever passes for one) like some modern-day Nora Desmond. They think I need time to "prepare." But that's like cramming for an exam at the last minute. By then it's too late. At T-minus 30, I'm either good to go or I'm not.

I like watching and listening to the audience, getting a sense of their energy or lack thereof. They can be boisterous or subdued. It doesn't matter. I take them where I find them. It's like plugging in and getting connected to the here and now. I will admit there are times when it doesn't matter how long I stand there, I can't make any connection at all. But I still have to get on stage and do the job. I suppose that's what separates the Newbies from the Pros; the ability to stand and deliver no matter your mood or that of the audience.

If the pre-show vibe I feel coming from a crowd is like food, then what I felt that night onboard the Carnival Destiny was a full-course feast filled with all my favorites, and sweet potato pie for dessert. Why was this show so particularly tasty?

While I do have fans, I'm still at that stage of my career, where more often than not, people see me by chance. They're going to a comedy club or special event, and I just happen to be there. Win-win. On this night, however, they were coming to see me, specifically. That's different. I suppose that's what separates the Pros from the Celebrities. That is what fame feels like. That is what most performing artists are working towards. And it was delicious. I'll take another helping of that, please, thank you very much.

Of course, I still had to deliver the goods. But it was nice not to have to start from zero, to have the deck stacked in my favor, to have the game be mine to lose. That can and does happen for Newbies, Pros, and Celebs alike. In American football they call it "any given Sunday." You can have a bad show in an ideal setting and a great show in a dump. That's the horror and the beauty of it. And this night was gorgeous. As fabulous as it felt though I knew not to get too comfortable. Audience love is not unconditional love. It's magical but fleeting. But if they keep coming, I'll keep bringing.

Barefoot Stand-Up

When I go on-stage to perform, I like to dress up; nothing ostentatious, but neat, clean, and stylish. But one night I'd been traveling all day and I was tired. The outfit I put on was nice, but when it came time for the shoes I just couldn't face putting on a pair of pumps. The heel was a respectable two and a half inches high, but cramming my toes into a pair of black satin, pointy-toed sling-backs seemed like cruel and unusual punishment.

I've often fantasized about performing barefoot. I saw Sade do it in her 1993 PBS concert and I loved it. She looked both, classy and earthy standing there in a slinky, white, Morticia Addams–style gown, her perfectly manicured toes peeking out from the bottom of her dress. Glancing at my own toes, I saw that my week-old pedicure still looked decent. Was tonight the night? Was I brave enough? Could I walk out on-stage barefoot and tell jokes?

And then my eyes fell upon my slippers, a brand new recently purchased pair with the price tag still attached. These weren't of the big-pink-bunny variety, complete with nose, whiskers, and floppy ears. These looked like ballet slippers. All black, top and bottom, they blended in perfectly with my pants. And, best of all, the slippers were foam padded. "Oh yes," my feet seemed to say. So, I slipped on my slippers and yes, my feet felt fabulous, the best thing short of a full-on foot massage.

"No, this is crazy," I thought. "I can't wear slippers on-stage! It's unprofessional."

"Who says?" my tired toes chimed in. "They look good. No one will mind. No one will even notice."

I took a gander at myself in the full-length mirror to see if my eyes could settle the argument between my head and my feet, and it became four against one. To the casual observer it looked like I was wearing black flats.

My mind — finally on team comfort — even reasoned that I'd give a better performance if my feet didn't hurt. Weather wasn't a factor either since I was performing on a cruise ship. The showroom was just one deck down. And so I walked out of my room, my heels left behind like bewildered sinners after The Rapture. In fact, my shoes remained packed and untouched during the entire trip. I relished the compliments I received on my "cute shoes" as women seductively stumbled around the Promenade Deck in strappy stilettos while the ship swayed from port to port.

For my next show I may not bother packing shoes at all, which puts me one step closer to performing Sade-style, in my bare feet. The stage, of course, will have to be foam padded.

ON THE ROAD

It's very important to travel. You have to get out of your zip code, go to a different Wal-Mart. It really broadens you.

THE DESERT IS NO PLACE FOR NEAT FREAKS

Entertaining the troops in the Middle East during Operation Enduring Freedom back in 2002 was a once-in-a-lifetime opportunity. Spending 30 days on bases in Afghanistan, Pakistan, and Saudi Arabia was alternately thrilling and exhausting. When it was over, I assumed I'd never do it again. But my wanderlust got the better of me and — thanks to Armed Forces Entertainment — off I went to Iraq: five comics, nine bases, 10 days. Amazing!

Military audiences are some of the best I've ever performed for, hands down. Given the stressful environment and the dangerous jobs they do, the soldiers are highly appreciative of the brief respite they get when attending the performances of visiting entertainers. We are treated like gold.

One of the coolest things was getting to bunk in Saddam Hussein's hunting lodge. The U.S. military converted this mini palace into a hotel complete with dining area, gym, and Internet. Aside from the bunk beds, the lodge was lavishly furnished with the gaudiest Victorian furniture I've ever seen. It's proof that being a wealthy, maniacal dictator doesn't automatically confer one with a sense of style.

Because of the upcoming Iraqi elections — which were not expected to be calm or peaceful — ground transportation was out of the question. So, we traveled to shows by Black Hawk helicopter. At $10 million a pop, it's a very expensive taxi. They're great for short trips but anything longer than 30 minutes requires earplugs, buns of steel, and long johns. Black Hawks have a four-man crew:

Pilot, copilot, and two gunners for whom the windows stay open, giving new meaning to the phrase freezing your ass off. I'd love to be able to tell my grandchildren about this trip, but I'm not sure if my eggs will ever completely thaw.

A couple of the bases we visited were all male. "It's Raining Men" looped through my mind so often I probably owe royalties. We not only have a well-trained military but a good-looking one as well; Selective Service indeed. I love the smell of testosterone in the morning.

I'm always stunned though by how young our soldiers are. We met a baby-faced 17-year old who should have been playing video games at home, not war games in the desert. I wondered if it was too late to call his mom and get him grounded. Having acne and an M-16 just feels wrong but on the other hand, who would be intimidated by a fighting force of 50-year-olds? It's not that they're past their prime; they're just past the point in their lives when they can live on Pop Tarts and energy drinks without dire digestive consequences. That's not the kind of surge anyone has in mind.

While performing for the troops is a rewarding experience, it's not for everybody. It can be physically and emotionally draining, and requires a great deal of patience and flexibility. Even though my second tour had more amenities than the first, there were still the issues of body armor, helmets, bunk beds, carb-heavy food, and sand. The vast amount of the latter was a bit of a shock. Sure, we have beaches in New York but by comparison, our sand is more like concrete with low self-esteem.

Suffice it to say the desert is no place for neat freaks. My inner Felix Unger was having a nervous breakdown. The soldiers were carrying guns and I wanted to carry a Swiffer. Thank goodness for baby wipes. I doubt I'd do well in the military.

"Where's your weapon, soldier?"

"Wrapped in plastic, sir!"

The military uses a 24-hour clock:

0900 (oh-nine hundred) hours is 9 a.m.

1200 (twelve hundred) hours is noon.

1300 (thirteen hundred) hours is 1p.m.

Many of our shows were at 1900 hours (7 p.m.) but for me, 1900 isn't a time of day. It's a year and 2300 sounds like we're meeting in the future.

Math is not my strong suit. Consequently I never really knew what time it was. Factor in the challenge of keeping in touch with my family in New York on Eastern Standard Time, and I was constantly adding 12, subtracting eight, and regretting not taking a quantum physics class when I had the chance. Where's Stephen Hawking when you need him?

And then were the porta potties. If you're afflicted with Archie Bunker Syndrome — that is, you can only go to the bathroom in your own home — then scratch trekking through the Middle East off your bucket list. In America, the porcelain throne is standard equipment, but in that part of the world you're just as likely to use a hole in the ground. I saw such a hole in the floor in the women's bathroom in the Kuwait International Airport and I felt my colon hermetically seal itself.

Thankfully, most of the bases had indoor plumbing, but indoor doesn't mean good. One base had one bathroom for each ... uh ... function. There was a Number One Bathroom and a Number Two Bathroom. You had to decide ahead of time what you were going to do and stick to it; no changing your mind at the last minute. Who's got that kind of gastrointestinal fortitude? Do they teach that in Basic Training?

America's presence in the Middle East is fraught with tension. Why are we there? When are we leaving? What are we fighting for: oil, democracy, cultural superiority? Perhaps it all comes down to plumbing. One of the most basic freedoms and pleasures in life is being able to, shall we say, fire at will in a safe and clean environment. When you can't do that, the terrorists win. I'm proud that the laughs we brought to the troops and hope it helped their hearts, minds, and colons.

Hotel Room Sign in Singapore:

'It's Illegal To Feed The Monkeys.'

So I fed a squirrel and he fed the monkeys.

WELCOME TO SINGAPORE

My work entertaining the troops took me to Changi Naval Base in Singapore. Who wouldn't want to visit the country that's featured in almost every episode of National Geographic's *Locked Up Abroad?* "Tune in next week when an American goes to Singapore and does something stupid. Again." Do you remember, Michael Fay, the American kid who got caned for vandalism back in 1994? Singapore is not soft on crime.

The customs and immigration form I filled out on the flight said, in big bold letters, **"DEATH TO DRUG TRAFFICKERS!"** Not a lot of wiggle room. They don't care why you're dealing drugs: **DEATH**! They don't care about what kind of childhood you had: **DEATH**! There's no plea bargain, reduced sentence, or time off for good behavior from **DEATH**!

Singapore is called a "fine" city not only because of its commitment to cleanliness but because of the myriad of seemingly innocuous offenses for which one can be . . . well . . . fined.

Eating and drinking in public? Fine!

Jay walking? Fine!

Spitting? Fine!

Gum Chewing? Fine!

Singapore is sweating the small stuff.

It was tough to refrain from jay walking, the birthright of every self-respecting native New Yorker, but no gum chewing? That was difficult. I chewed gum all through Catholic school and never got nabbed. If the nuns caught you in the act of mastication they made you put the gum on your nose. Yeah, that's exactly what Jesus would do. But I've been out of school for a while and have grown accustomed to chewing. Singapore is a bit more punitive than Catholic school with a $1,000 fine and possible imprisonment. You're not even allowed to bring gum into the country. The penalty for gum trafficking: **Death!** No, not really but the $10,000 fine is killer.

So, unwilling to risk a *Locked Up Abroad* situation I divested myself of my gum stash. I considered hiding a pack or two in my suitcase, but I worried that they might have gum-sniffing dogs at the airport. My dog, Rolie, could easily do that job. He's the reason I've had to stop leaving my purse on the floor. On more than one occasion I've seen him neck deep in my bag like a pig rooting for truffles. And yes, he's figured out how to work the zipper. He's a crafty little cur.

Even if I had managed to smuggle gum into Singapore, I would have been too afraid to chew it. Are the cops on the lookout for people with minty fresh breath? Does Singapore have chew cams strategically placed around the city to catch careless bubble blowers in the act? I just couldn't risk it. And besides, Altoids aren't so bad once you stop being curious as to why they're so "curiously strong."

But I half hoped half feared that I'd be approached by an

illegal gum dealer: "Hey Girl, whatchu want? I got Bubble Yum, Bubblicious, Hubba Bubba! I'll hook you up, Boo!" But just my luck, he would've been an undercover cop.

To be clear, fascist dentists aren't running the show in Singapore. They're more like overzealous neat freaks. The no gum-chewing edict hopes to curb those who would spit out their gum in the street rather than throw it in the garbage. But it just goes to show, weapon of mass destruction is a relative term. Perhaps Singapore never considered sending troops to Iraq because Saddam Hussein wasn't stockpiling Juicy Fruit. He didn't have any weapons either but that's another story.

People who practice alternative medicine say that animals can smell disease in the human body. That's why I have a dog. If he sniffs my butt and doesn't growl, I'm good. Instead of the canary in coalmine it's the cocker spaniel in the colon.

HANGING WITH HUGO IN THE FORME

It's easy for the Fourth of July to go by in a blur of beer, barbeque, and fireworks, but I never thought I'd have the best Fourth ever 4,625 miles away from American shores. My recent tour for Armed Forces Entertainment culminated with a final show at Camp Bondsteel in Kosovo. If you're wondering where that is, think The Balkans, or for you history buffs, The Ottoman Empire.

Currently, Kosovo – comprised largely of Albanians – is one of the poorer countries of the European Union. On the 45-minute drive from the airport in Prishtina (the capital) we saw a lot of houses without windows making the country look like a nation under renovation. "People live there," said our MWR (Morale, Welfare & Recreation) Host. "They have to start paying taxes when the windows go in." So, if you hate doing windows and paying taxes, Prishtina may be the place for you.

Be warned though, the commute's a bit rough especially if you fly Air Berlin; the Greyhound of the Skies without the charm. Instead of passengers boarding by rows or groups the gate agent said, "on your mark, get set, go." At least that's what I think she said. I can't be sure since the one and only announcement was made in German. I took Spanish in high school, so my knowledge of German begins and ends with schnitzel and Hitler, and too much of either is not good for you.

So my tour mates and I took our cue it was time to leave when the boarding area erupted into a marathon with carry-ons. The running of the bulls in Spain now seems tame by comparison.

The next day, however, was July Fourth and MWR at Bondsteel put on an absolutely fabulous Big Ass Barbeque. Although far from home, the menu was full of familiar fare: hamburgers, hot dogs, chicken, ribs, potato and macaroni salads, bratwurst . . . Okay, bratwurst isn't very American, but no complaints from moi, not when there was also sweet tea. Wunderbar!

Festivities included volleyball, vendors, music, a base talent show and, of course, comedy. I was a little worried about the show since Bondsteel is a mixed base with both U.S. and NATO soldiers. Much to my delight though, the Danish soldiers enjoyed my Swedish massage jokes.

After the comedy show we were treated to the wrap-up of the Camp Bondsteel Talent Competition. I'm not a flag-waving xenophobe, but I'd be lying if I said I didn't tear up when Specialist Raul Sanchez opened the show by singing The Star-Spangled Banner. What a voice! And he wasn't even a finalist! The three soldiers, who were, took the stage with a level of talent and showmanship that put *American Idol* to shame. Respectively, the men sang, "Hello," "Pour Some Sugar on Me," and the winner did a rendition of "Sexual Healing" that would have made Marvin Gaye gay.

The only things missing from the BBQ were alcohol and fireworks. I know I just lost some you hard-core swillers, but Camp Bondsteel is a dry base. The good news was you could have all the non-alcoholic beer your bladder could handle. It was jokingly referred to as "Near Beer," tasting nowhere near it at all.

I missed seeing fireworks, but I could certainly understand the reason for the ban. On a base sporting posters of what to look for in a land mine, explosions as entertainment weren't a good idea. The combination of alcohol and fireworks usually doesn't end well, as I'm sure you cherry bomb amputees out there will agree.

Dog Lover that I am, I enjoyed meeting Hugo, one of three members of the camp's K-9 Unit. You wouldn't know it to look at him, but he was eight-years-old. That's geriatric for a military dog, but I think Camp Bondsteel was Hugo's retirement gig. Clearly the camp favorite, he couldn't walk more than three feet without someone coming over to chat, pet him, or give him a treat.

As we dined at the BBQ with MWR Host & Camp Mom, Renee Favors, we watched her share pieces of chicken with Hugo. When she wasn't feeding him fast enough, he barked loudly as if to say, "Hurry up, woman! I'm not getting any younger!"

Hugo came to the comedy show, sat right in the front row, and fell asleep. I didn't take it personally. He'd had a really busy day. Who wouldn't need a snooze after all that chicken?

After the show, the Base Commander called all the comedians back out on stage to thank us for our service and gave each of us a plaque of appreciation and a set of commemorative dog tags, my first ever. It was a lovely bonus considering that they already had me at sweet tea.

Hugo was awake and alert for this part of the presentation so I'm guessing the dog tags were his idea.

A woman's left breast is usually bigger than the right because it's closer to the heart. That's how you can tell who the cold-hearted bitches are.

EYE BALLING MY BOOBIES

I'm not a buxom babe and I'm at peace with that. I wasn't always. Puberty was a trial. Despite reading Judy Blume's *Are You There God, It's Me, Margaret?* and faithfully executing its famous exercises: – repeat after me if you remember – "I must, I must, I must increase my bust!" my little cupcakes seemed genetically preordained to be unobtrusive. They are a respectable 34B instead of the sought after 36C or dare I dream, D.

I once went to Victoria Secret to get my bust measured, to make sure I was wearing the right bra. I was secretly hoping they'd find something I'd missed. The good news: Yes, I was wearing the wrong size bra. The bad news: It was too big for me. According to the evil Victoria Secret measuring tape I'm a double A. Stand back everybody. I'm packing batteries. When I was in school going from a "B" to an "A" was a good thing. What can I say but fie on you, Victoria, and a pox on your secret!

Let me be clear. I'm not flat chested. But I know, from a purely esthetic point of view, my bust is not the main attraction, but an integral part of the total package. At best I've got a couple of good team players. So it was with total surprise when I caught a man in the act of full-on ogling my boobies. I was on tour in Europe with a day off in between shows. Our hosts were kind enough to take us to Liege in Belgium to shop at the open-air market.

As I walked past an older gentleman sitting at an outdoor café, he casually looked me up and down and then his gaze fell abruptly to my chest, and stayed there, riveted. It was so far out of the realm of my personal experience and it happened so fast that I wasn't sure it happened at all.

I would have dismissed it completely had a friend not been there to witness it. I turned to her with my, "Did that just happen?" face and she responded with her, "Yes, it did" face. She too seemed surprised and impressed. There was a hint of, "You go, girl" in the arch of her eyebrows. I was content to let the incident pass, filed away under random acts of weird when one block later it happened again.

What the deuce? One's an anomaly. Two's a pattern. But why? I wanted to ask but didn't have the nerve to say, "Excuse me, sir? Why are you eye balling my boobies?" I also have no idea how to say "boobies" in French, Dutch, or German, Belgium's three main languages.

Perhaps Europeans don't share the American fascination for freakishly large breasts, preferring instead more natural proportions. This could correspond to the smaller food portions Europeans mysteriously seem capable of surviving on. Apparently, they don't supersize their food or their women. Let's hear it for European sophistication.

It would be fair to say that I was both tickled and offended. Well, according to my inner feminist I "should" be offended but this was clearly at odds with my inner adolescent who, at the age of 18, was depressed when a much hoped for last-minute breast growth spurt didn't materialize.

But the older I get, the more I find that real life resides in the undulating shades of gray. In other words, yes, objectification is wrong, but may she who has not gazed appreciatively upon the chiseled abs of the Abercrombie & Fitch models cast the first stone. Is there a time and place to openly appreciate what is pleasing to the eye? Apparently, it's any random afternoon in Belgium.

Note to self: look into dual citizenship.

*I live in a really bad neighborhood.
Earth.*

PUNCH LINES & POMPOMS

"You're going where?" my Parents said. They had confused and weary expressions on their faces when I told them I was going on a short (three-day) tour with Armed Forces Entertainment to perform for the troops doing humanitarian work in Haiti. Several questions brewed on their brows:

Didn't you just get home from Iraq?

Can't you just tell jokes in seedy nightclubs like a normal comedian?

Do we still have the authority to ground you?

Yes, no, and no.

Before I could baby-wipe all the Iraqi dust off my combat boot–style Converses, friend and fellow comedian Carole Montgomery called and asked if I wanted to entertain the troops in Haiti. Not one to let the pages in my passport go to waste, I said yes.

The earthquake and the plight of the Haitian people have faded from the front pages of newspapers and web sites, but humanitarian efforts were still going on. As part of Operation Unified Response, several branches of the United States military went to Haiti's aid in the aftermath of the devastating January 12, 2010, earthquake that crippled the capital of Port au Prince.

Down from a 21,000 high during the thick of the crisis, those who remained in Haiti were busy relocating people to safer areas ahead of the coming rainy and hurricane seasons. The conditions were austere. The heat and humidity were debilitating. The boredom was palpable. At the end of the day workers didn't return to home and hearth, but to camp and tent.

Tent living is great because it quickly reminds you of all the things you take for granted, like a comfortable bed and privacy. The women's tent sported cots for beds and bed sheets pinned to nylon clothesline for walls. On the plus side, our tent was one of the few with air conditioning, which kept us cool and mosquito free. I soon learned, however, that while 60 degrees feels good when you've just walked in from the heat, it feels downright frigid in the middle of the night when you're trying to sleep. I zipped my sleeping bag up past my ears to block out the sound of Morpheus' chattering teeth.

The mosquito situation was serious enough to require us to take anti-malaria medication. Malaria? Seriously? I'm so spoiled. In the northeastern United States we've pretty much hunted, trapped, and sprayed our bugs into submission; roaches notwithstanding. But in Haiti the bugs are bold. I think one asked me out.

In addition to the mosquitoes, there was Maggie, a beautiful, light brown, mixed-breed dog. She was nothing but skin and bones when the soldiers arrived, but the rules were very clear: No Pets. So nobody owned Maggie, nobody fed her, and this same group of nobodies bought her a flea collar. Nobody was also working on bringing her back to the United States. Maggie it seemed owned everybody.

Three-minute combat showers were the order of the day. I

know. That's barely enough time to sing all the verses of the "Umbrella" song. But I didn't mind a short shower especially since the water was cold. I didn't mean to take a cold shower but the water never warmed up during the three minutes I was shivering under it. I wished I could have skipped it but the living conditions made good hygiene super-über critical. I didn't enjoy smelling like a combination of sweat, bug repellent, and hand sanitizer. But on the bright side, a cold shower makes you ask yourself critical life questions like:

I don't smell that bad do I?

Can I just use baby wipes?

Can I get away with just Febreezing myself?

Yes, no, and no.

The military made sure we were well fed. We never went hungry, but it wasn't fancy. We had at least one cooked meal supplemented with MREs (meals ready to eat), heater meals, cold cereal, and assorted snack food. I lived on apples, V-8, and Gardetto Chips while dreaming of yogurt, salad, and meat I could visibly identify.

I don't know how they managed it, but the camp's ladies-only porta potty was beautiful. Like *Doctor Who's* TARDIS it seemed bigger on the inside. It was well lit, smelled good, and had an ample supply of multi-ply Charmin toilet paper, proving once again that where there's a woman, there's a way.

In addition to Carole I had the pleasure of working with

three of the Miami Dolphins cheerleaders. They made up the other half of what was dubbed The Hijinks and High Kicks Tour. In the interests of full disclosure I have to admit that my inner teenager who never got to be a cheerleader did not want to like these women. Something primordial from the dark side of my brain assumed they'd be no more than vapid wastrels. Apparently my dark side has an extensive vocabulary.

But these women did not fit the stereotype at all. Yes, they were young and beautiful, but they were also smart, talented, organized, and hard working. They very much impressed me with their college degrees, full-time jobs, and post-cheer leading career plans already in the works. It also helped that I was mistaken once or twice for being one of the cheerleaders. This went a long way toward placating my inner insecure adolescent.

On this very short trip we did three shows, all outside, atop flatbed trucks. The last show was at the U.S. embassy, which gave us the chance to drive through the very crowded streets of Port au Prince. We saw the poverty mixed in with the damage, so much devastation afflicted on those who could least afford it.

It was heartbreaking to see the Haitian children begging outside the embassy gate, but we weren't allowed to give them any money. We were told it would end up going to their "handlers," the men who sent the kids out to beg like real-life Oliver Twists.

Humor can't heal everything, but for a moment I wished that I could tell jokes in Creole. "Bonswa! Sak Pase?" The children reminded me of what I take for granted most: my family; my amazing Parents who raised me to follow my dreams, but are sometimes terrified of where that takes me. "You're going where?" They asked me that every day for a week leading up to my trip as if either the answer or my mind would change. I'm sure they'd have been a lot happier if I'd said I was going to seek fame and fortune in Los Angeles, but L.A. scares me in a way that war zones and natural disasters don't.

One year it snowed so badly in Toronto they had to get the army to help dig them out. Seriously? Canada has an army?

CHILLIN' IN WISCONSIN

If Hell freezes over I think it'll feel like winter in Wisconsin. On a trip to the badger state, I had to rent a car. The rental company required that I sign a Cold Weather Waiver stating that if the car didn't start – due to the weather – it wasn't their fault. Not only would I still have to pay for the rental, I'd also have to pay for the car to be towed from wherever I'd left it. Oh dear.

When it was time to return the car, the Weather Channel informed me that it was a clear and sunny minus 13 degrees with a wind chill of minus 20. Suddenly car abandonment didn't seem like such a bad idea.

Wind chill never meant much to me. I'd always assumed it was something weathermen invented to make themselves look busy. But in Wisconsin, wind chill is serious business. It's enough to warrant school closures and dire warnings that going out will guarantee you a case of fanny frostbite.

I toyed with the idea of staying in bed. The Port Zedler Motel on Port Washington Road in Mequon, Wisconsin, may not have been much to look at, but it had cable and heat.

I dressed in layers - thermal underwear, thermal socks, jeans, turtleneck, sweatshirt, fur-lined gloves, hat, two scarves, ear muffs, Timberland boots, L.L. Bean coat - and against my better judgment, I headed out.

Going outside was like stepping into a black hole. I couldn't feel the wind blowing, but the cold was thick and heavy like a wet pair of jeans. It stung my eyes and it felt as if my contact lenses were freezing beneath my lids.

With the Weather Waiver upper most in my mind, I turned the key in the ignition. The car gasped and sputtered like a drowning man trying to come up for air. My heart froze, or perhaps it was just taking a cue from my contact lenses. "Oh no! Where am I gonna find a cab at 6:30 in the morning?" I turned the key again and I heard a few more gasps of protest. It was the car's way of saying, "C'mon lady, it's 20 below!"

I put my forehead down on the steering wheel as if to make the car understand that it was nothing personal, I simply had to get to the airport. On the third try the car started. Weather Waiver be damned!

The drive was relatively easy once I understood the Milwaukee driving philosophy: if you're lucky enough to get your car started, put the pedal to the metal, and don't stop until the spring thaw.

I made it to the airport, but the flight was delayed for over an hour due to mechanical difficulties caused, of course, by the weather. I guess the pilot had also signed the Cold Weather Waiver and was haggling over how much it would cost to get the plane towed to Pittsburgh.

AN AMERICAN
You're going to Alaska? What's the exchange rate?

ME
One to one.

GRANNY PANTIES

Thanks to stand-up comedy I've traveled to and performed in 46 of the 50 United States, plus Guam. I'm missing Alaska, Kentucky, Montana, and Washington, but under less than ideal circumstances I'm finally going to Alaska. By less than ideal circumstance I mean winter. I'll be doing shows at military bases in and around Anchorage and Fairbanks. I'm excited about getting closer to my goal of performing in all 50 states, but it's butting up against my desire to be comfortable and by comfortable, I mean warm.

I get cold easy. I carry a sweater in the summer because air conditioning is too oppressive for me. I begin donning hats and leggings in September. And if I had my way, my house would be a balmy 80 degrees from October to April, but I live with a white guy who begins wilting at 70.

I've been watching the Weather Channel, which by the way doesn't include Hawaii, Alaska, or Guam in its national forecast. Apparently we're to assume it's respectively hot, cold, and who cares. The more inclusive Weather.com told me the local temperature in Anchorage is about 20 degrees Fahrenheit. Okay, that's manageable. Fairbanks: Minus 30. MINUS THIRTY?!? Is that a typo?

I seriously began worrying that I wouldn't be warm enough. And by worry I mean panic. Everyone says it's best to dress in layers, but how practical is that? I buy clothes to fit me, not some bigger, outsized version of me. That would, however, be a handy excuse: "I'm not fat, I'm layering."

In preparation I've been stocking up on thermal underwear, wool socks, and hand warmers. This is literally the time to cover your ass. So, no, I won't be packing a thong. Alaska in January is a time for the granny panties. I need maximum skin coverage. At this point, I even regret shaving my armpits.

I'm worried now about my outerwear. Everybody, and by everybody I mean Google, says down coats are best. I thought I had one, but when I fished it out of the attic, the label read, "Lining: 100% polyester." Fantastic! I'll freeze to death but at least I'll be wrinkle free.

So that's how I found myself, three days before wheels up, trolling through The Burlington Coat Factory looking for something to fit over multiple layers but that didn't make me feel like the abominable snow man. To their credit, BCF had a lovely selection of coats but the down linings topped out at 60%. Surely a January jaunt to Alaska warrants 80% to 90%.

Shopaholic that I am, my attention soon wandered to a sexy, bright red, plastic rain coat that perfectly matched a handbag that I'd recently scored at Nine West for $10. Just as I began imagining how cute I'd look in the coat/bag combo, my Husband – who I brought along to keep me focused – whispered a gentle weather reminder: "Hey Baby: Minus 40 degrees, but the wind chill makes it feel like, FUCK!"

And we're back.

I don't know why I never realized it before, but trying on a coat inside the store is somewhat pointless. You can judge look and fit but not warmth. Wouldn't it make more sense to have an outdoor dressing room where you can try on a coat under more realistic conditions?

I eventually found a coat that has native New Yorker written all over it: black, full-length, and slightly tapered at the waist. It's no red raincoat, but I dare say it's stylish. While there's no standardized Zagat's-type rating for outerwear, a tag on the coat sleeve read:

"Garments made of ARCTIC WARMTH™ have been specially designed for comfort and heat retention to keep you warm during moderate physical activity such as walking during Canadian winters."

Translation, "Keep moving!" But that should be good enough for Alaska as well since it would have been part of Canada if Canada could have gotten her money together.

Oddly though, the makers of the coat still hedged their bets a bit:

"For best results with ARCTIC WARMTH™ it is recommended to dress in layers in extreme cold weather in order to ensure better heat conservation."

So much for "high tech fillers."

Luckily a cold snap in New York allowed me to field-test the coat. So far so good but 18 degrees in The Big Apple may not feel the same as 18 in The Big Chill. I hope I fair well in Fairbanks and by fair well I mean not end up a stylishly dressed ice sculpture.

America ranks the lowest in education but the highest in drug use. We can fix that. All we need to do is start the war on education. If it's anywhere as near successful as the war on drugs, we'd all be hooked on phonics.

DRUG TEST WAKEUP CALL

When the phone rang at 9:37 a.m. I knew the caller must have the wrong number. No one ever calls me in my cabin when I'm working onboard a cruise ship. I'm a comedian. They don't need me until showtime but I answered the phone anyway because that was the only way to make it stop ringing.

"Hello, Leighann?"

"Yes."

"It's the Assistant Cruise Director."

"Hey, what's up?"

"I'm sorry," he said, "You've been randomly selected for a drug test."

Silence.

He hurried on to say that the other comedian had been chosen as well as if this would somehow make it better. Then he said, "Security needs to see you in five minutes."

Five minutes? That bothered me more than being asked to take a drug test. I hate to be a stereotypical girly-girl, but if you want me to be somewhere in five minutes, you need to give me a 24-hour heads up.

"Sure," I mumbled and stumbled out of bed angry with myself. Had I gotten up to go work out when my alarm went off at 7 a.m. I might have missed this madness entirely. They would have had to chase me down as I made my rounds on the outdoor track.

I wasn't worried though. I can pass a drug test. What I may not be able to pass is a credit check. As I joke in my act:

"I don't drink, I don't smoke, I don't do drugs, but I will shop a bitch under the table."

I was still miffed. No one has the right to do drugs – unless the makers of those drugs have contributed enough money to the right political campaigns – but it felt like yet another boot heel firmly pressed down on the throat of my already severely constricted liberty.

I can understand testing people who work in critical areas. Handling money? Yes. Driving, flying, or piloting any kind of vehicle, vessel, or heavy machinery? Yes, yes, and yes. Caring for children? Yes, but I can certainly see how people in the caring professions could develop a drug habit.

But what is the value in drug testing performing artists? It would be wildly incorrect to say that all entertainers do drugs. Many of us in fact do not, but it's no secret that some believe drugs to be an integral part of their creative process. If drug testing had been common in the 80s, stand-up comedy might not exist today.

I'd never taken a drug test before, but if you've ever had to do lab work for the doctor the instruction is the same: pee in the cup. I've had varying degrees of success with this depending on the size of the provided receptacle. At one time the lab at my doctor's office only gave out thin, narrow test tubes. Let's just say from a flexibility, aim, and sight-line point of view it was challenging.

As if peeing on command for this random drug test wasn't degrading enough, I was told not to flush the toilet or to wash my hands. Why? It could interfere with the results of the test. So, we're no longer worrying about the Norovirus are we? That's the stomach virus that periodically breaks out on cruise ships treating sufferers to muscle aches, vomiting, and diarrhea. It led to hand sanitizing stations being installed everywhere with signs reminding you to frequently wash your hands, reminiscent of a viral duck and cover.

This non-flushing, non-hand washing directive violated my own personal code of cleanliness. I felt icky. So when I saw the security officer's walkie-talkie perched on the sink I wasn't allowed to use, I took a perverse pleasure in bringing it out to him with my very unwashed hands. The look of horrified thanks on his face was well worth it.

Yes, I know this was petty and yet it was also curiously satisfying. The only thing better would have been to urinate on the walkie-talkie directly but that crosses the line between passive-aggressive and aggressive-aggressive.

The most important lesson I learned in all this: Don't sleep past my alarm.

Whenever I go to Book Club, me and my friends always end up talking about our moms.
That's how Book Club turned into Wine Club.

HAVE WINE GLASS, WILL TRAVEL

I was a first-time faculty member at the Erma Bombeck Writers' Workshop (EBWW) and I left with a respectable amount of swag: tee shirt, tote bag, and my personal favorite, the commemorative wine glass. Let it not be said that the EBWW doesn't know its audience: Women who write, love wine; and lots of it. At the Thursday night dinner, the wine glasses had been delicately imprinted with "Erma Bombeck Writers' Workshop." Every woman in the room said to herself or one of her tablemates, "Oh, I am so stealing this."

But we didn't have to. They announced that the glasses were ours to keep. And there was a round of applause to go with our first round of drinks. But this was slightly disappointing since figuring out how to squeeze a wine glass into an evening clutch is half the fun. Figuring out how to get it home in my suitcase, not so much.

Me, who attempts to plan for every contingency, didn't have a spare sheet of bubble wrap and a box squirreled away in the corner of my carryon. But even if I did I was afraid that no matter how carefully I wrapped and positioned this delicate keepsake in my suitcase it would arrive home broken. And so, there I was strolling through the Dayton airport, plane ticket in one hand, wine glass in the other. And it wasn't even noon.

A few people at the airport looked at me approvingly as if to say, "Yeah! That's so awesome!" But others were shaking their heads and clearly thinking, "You really need to get your life together."

111

If I had been going straight home on a direct flight I might have braved the collective looks of derisive admiration, but I was going to be on two connecting flights to another gig. Ultimately I just wanted to get the glass home intact.

I went into the CNBC store just outside of security and asked if I could have a small plastic bag. I figured something was better than nothing. The cashier looked at my wine glass and said, "Oh that's beautiful. You need to wrap that." She reached under her register and produced tissue paper and tape, wrapped and double bagged it for me like Christmas elf! I was delighted and grateful.

I joined the TSA line with my concealed wine-ware. And I didn't feel like such a wandering lush but I also didn't feel nearly as cool. I now see the appeal of the flask. Perhaps they'll be giving those away at the next workshop.

When I was a kid my parents didn't want to have the "sex"
talk with me. And now I don't want to have the "death" talk
with them. I found out from my friends.
I'm hoping they find out from theirs.

MY MAYA

Well, it's disingenuous to claim Maya Angelou as mine, but don't we all kinda feel that way? She sat next to me once in first class on an early-morning flight. I can't tell you where I was going to or coming from; most likely a comedy gig. I really don't know. All I remember with any clarity is that I was sitting next to Maya Angelou.

I had boarded early and was ensconced in the window seat selfishly hoping the one next to me would remain open. I looked up and saw Her coming down the aisle. At first I thought, "Hmm... she looks familiar." I think this was my brain's way of protecting me from taking in all at once the reality of who I was seeing.

Alice Walker? Cicely Tyson? And then... "It's Her. It's Maya Angelou!"

I stared – well, I tried not to and failed – as She walked up, stopped at the empty seat next to me, and began sitting down. I'm not schizophrenic, but the voices in my head became a screaming mob:

Stop staring.

I'm not staring.

Yes, you are.

Okay I'm staring.

Well stop it. You're being creepy.

Am not.

Are too.

Are you gonna say something?

What? No. It's Maya Angelou!

Exactly! It's Maya Angelou! You can't be rude.

But maybe She wants to be left alone.

Just say, "Hi." Don't try to sit in Her lap.

Fine.

Fine.

Okay.

Okay.

Well hurry up and say something before it gets weird.

I took a deep breath to get my heart out of my throat and said, "Good morning."

She said, "Good morning."

And that simple exchange of pleasantries was all I could handle. That's right. I essentially get paid to talk for a living and now I couldn't. I had no words at least none on the outside. On the inside it was the Tower of Babel:

Oh. My. God.

She spoke to me. Did you hear that? She spoke to me!

See, that wasn't so bad.

I know.

Should I say something else?

Oh for the love of god, no.

Why not?

Because you'll embarrass us!

And so I sat there quietly reading my book. And by reading I mean staring at type on a page. Don't ask me what the book was. I have no idea. All I remember is that I was sitting next to Maya Freaking Angelou. How I wish I had been reading *And Still I Rise* so the voices in my head could've debated about asking for Her autograph.

A flight attendant came by and asked us if we wanted anything to drink. Without missing a beat Ms. Angelou said, "I'll have a vodka and orange juice."

The voices in my head said, *Well, damn. Is that why the caged bird sings?*

And it wasn't even 10 a.m.

As the flight got underway The Phenomenal Woman took out Her laptop and the voices said: *Oh My God Maya Angelou has a laptop?*

Of course She had a laptop. But somehow I thought She crafted Her brilliance with a feather quill and parchment. And then I thought:

Maya Angelou is gonna write a poem right here, right now, while She's next to me! Is this really happening?

This is happening!

I had to see what She was writing. I just had to. You understand that don't you? And so, as nonchalantly as I could (which means not at all) I shifted my position in my seat so I could see Her computer screen from the corner of my left eye. And that's when I saw that The Maya Angelou was playing solitaire.

You heard me. Solitaire.

And just like that she was transformed into a real person; a human being. My Maya. True, the vodka and orange juice before noon should've clued me in, but I'm a slow learner. I eased back into a comfortable position in my seat and the voices were quiet for the rest of the trip.

And now that My Maya has taken her final flight, her seat next to me while vacant will never be empty.

Good night, My Maya. We'll miss you. Safe travels.

BACKSTAGE

I'm uncomfortable with sexting. That's the kind of thing that can come back and bite you in the ass. Especially if you send a picture of somebody biting you in the ass.
#VanessaWilliams

A DAY IN THE LIFE OF A STAND-UP COMIC

I was waiting for the subway and a young woman with an expensive camera introduced herself as a Columbia University graduate student in its photojournalism program and asked permission to take my picture. If it was a scam – and I always think everything's a scam – it sounded like a good one so I said, yes. When my train came and we were about to part ways I gave her my business card hoping she'd send me one of the pictures but equally sure I'd never hear from her again. But she emailed me that night and asked if I would be the subject of her day-in-the-life class project. Again, I said, yes.

Part of me wanted to say no because honestly a day-in-the-life of yours truly isn't that interesting, especially that particular day. I wasn't dashing off to the airport. I had no auditions, podcasts, radio shows, or TV shoots. It wasn't even laundry day. Sure, I had a show later that night but during the day I was just writing. But she said that was fine. So we met at a coffee shop in Harlem – since I wasn't inviting a stranger to my home – and she spent most of the day photographing me with my nose in a book looking like I was doing nothing. Boring; or so I thought until I posted one of the pictures.

In the photo I'm working on my Set Book. (A comedian's set book is like an athlete's playbook; a singer's songbook; a painter's sketchbook). My Set Book began as hand-written notes on index cards, then in marble notebooks, then on loose leaf, and today is a 200 plus-page Word document (with a 26-page table of contents) that when printed double-sided on three-hole punched paper goes to live in My Big Red Binder. A Samuel Taylor Coleridge quote on the cover says: "People of humor are always in some degree people of genius."

My Set Book contains the jokes I'm doing now (my set), new material I'm working on (grouped thematically to enhance pattern recognition), random ideas to be developed (alphabetized by key word), and old ideas that I've tired of, outgrown, are in need of rethinking, or – clutch the pearls – deleting. It all goes in the book and I periodically print it out because seeing it on paper is different than seeing it on a computer screen. I then edit, tweak, and write new material using different colored pens in red, blue, black, green, and purple ink. Because I went to Catholic School and can't help myself, the red pen is for corrections. Blue and black are for notes and the longhand development of new ideas. Green indicates material to be moved and paired with other ideas. Purple is just because.

And in case you're wondering, I like my pens like I like my men: big and bold. When I write it's with a strong, heavy hand. I like making a physical impression on the paper. It's like the real world manifestation of the force and weight of what I'm thinking. So no, a fine point pen just doesn't do it for me. But I abstain from the writing versus typing debate. I am equally comfortable doing both. I guess that makes me ambi-technical. Why do I have to choose? Why does anybody? The only choice should be using whatever works best for you. And so through the magic of The Cloud my digital Set Book is always with me and yet, there are times when toting around My Big Red Binder and its retinue of pens feels right too.

I'm a big proponent of making technology serve the art. I record all my shows, sometimes video but always audio. Every one. Every time. Why? Why not? I didn't name my iPhone Mama's Little Tax Deduction for nothing. The note pad app is the cocktail napkin that will never be accidentally thrown away. Dictation is the butterfly net that captures the ephemeral notions born in my brain and later birthed into bits, blogs, books, or whatever. They'll let me know what they want to be when they grow up. When an idea presents itself all it wants from you, initially, is to say: "Yes, I see you. Yes, I hear you. Yes, I got you, Boo."

Then you feed and nurture it with your time and attention. Technology is just a tool to help you say yes. An idea should never be lost for want of pen and paper.

I used to feel self-conscious about my Set Book. Even though other comedians were often complimentary I suspected that I was being judged and maybe even mocked for my methods. Until one day I realized that I didn't care. Everybody's creative process is different. Mine has evolved over time. It works for me and that's all that matters.

And so, it turns out that the photo of me doing nothing was actually something. If a picture is worth a thousand words then this one is worth 50,609 give or take. Silly me though, I only posted the picture because I had the crazy idea that I was looking kinda cute that day. (Just say, yes.)

My healthcare plan is hope and hand sanitizer.

AMERICA'S NEXT TOP (HIV) MODEL?

I have an agent who sends me out on auditions for on-camera commercials and voice-overs. Recently they sent me to my first print audition; a pleasant surprise, since I'm not a model. Well-meaning friends and a few industry people have suggested I go out for print work, but quiet as it's kept, I don't photograph well.

"Pshaw," you say. "I've seen your headshots." Yes, they're good, but it's agony from start to finish. To be fair, it's not the photographer's fault. The vicious cycle begins with me: I don't think I photograph well ergo I'm not comfortable in front of the camera. My discomfort and all physical flaws — real and imagined — show up in the shots. I then end up sifting through tons of awful photos just to find the one that doesn't make me cringe.

I tell this to photographers all the time. At first they don't believe me. Then they start taking photos and fall strangely quiet. This usually means they're trying to find the best way to tell me about the wonders of Photoshop.

Sometimes this bothers me, but I'm learning to live with the idea that I'm one of those people who is most beautiful live and in the moment. I think this is preferable to having a picture that looks a lot better than I do. When you meet people who've only seen your fab photo they can't always hide their shock and disappointment at the disparity. It's so much nicer to hear, "Wow, you look way better in person."

My first print audition turned out to be for a product

called Lexiva, a medication that treats HIV infection. I heard my agent mention this on the phone but it didn't register until I was asked to sign a waiver stating that if I was hired, people may assume I am HIV positive even if I'm not. This concerned me but I figured it would be an opportunity to get over my "I don't photograph well" complex and get some print audition experience. I don't think watching *America's Next Top Model* counts.

The session was brief. The photographer sat me down under the lights, asked for four looks, snapped a few shots, and I was out the door. Looking at all the Serious Model Types who went in before and after me, I didn't think I stood a chance.

I was surprised when my agent called to tell me I was on first refusal. Figures. I seem to have a knack for doing commercials for products I don't use:

Century 21: Not in the market for a house.

Toyota Highlander: I own a Honda.

Lean Cuisine: I prefer home cooking.

US Cellular: I've got T-Mobile.

Elexa: The Female Condom. I'm sorry. I firmly – no pun intended – believe that a man should buy his own.

With my track record I'm surprised I haven't done an ad for Lexus.

Now suddenly the waiver I'd signed and what it meant felt a little more serious. What if I did the shoot and my face appeared on billboards all across America advertising an HIV medication? What if people really did assume I was HIV positive? I wonder if other actors have reservations about doing commercials or print work for drugs like Lexiva or even Valtrex (herpes) or Cialis (erectile dysfunction). How many of the agency's regulars said no when they found out what the product was? This would certainly explain why I'd gotten such an out-of-the-blue phone call.

Why not just take the money and run? Does it matter what strangers think? Personal goals and artistic integrity aside, a successful career in entertainment by its very nature depends a great deal on what strangers think. It's disingenuous to pretend otherwise.

That leaves friends and family. It shouldn't matter what they think because they love you and know the truth, right? Well, a few years ago my Husband did a print campaign for a diabetes medication. The campaign was targeted toward the medical community. He doesn't have diabetes, but that didn't stop our family doctor from assuming he did after seeing his face on the literature.

So, yeah, I'm a little concerned that doing a print ad for an HIV drug will make people think I'm HIV positive. Am I being shallow? Is my attitude perpetuating the climate of misunderstanding and insensitivity for the people who are indeed living with HIV? If my own vanity and insecurity leads me to turn this job down, am I giving up the opportunity to do my part in battling a disease that disproportionately affects my community and my gender?

These are uncomfortable questions I didn't expect to face

on a simple print audition. But ultimately, I'd expended all this mental anguish over a job I didn't get. My agent called to tell me someone else booked it. The decision was made for me, and yet I still wrestle with "what if."

Deep down I know that if they had hired me, those would be the best photos I'd ever taken. They'd have to be. If the goal is to sell medication, the manufacturer wants the people in the pictures to look supremely happy and healthy. At last, I'd look way better in print than I ever could in person, because that's how Mr. Murphy and his law work.

I would need a pit crew of makeup artists to maintain that look; otherwise I'd seem ill by comparison. And then people really would begin to wonder and whisper about my health.

ME
I'll have a hard shell taco, no cheese.

HER
No cheese?

ME
No cheese.

HER
You still want lettuce and meat?

ME
No, I want an empty taco.
I'm having an existential dinner.

SHITTY TIPPERS, SURLY SERVICE

It was a good gig: dinner and a show. For comedians this means getting a meal and money to perform. There are some gigs that feed you in lieu of compensation, but this was a double header. What was really nice was not being limited to the bar menu. That's the menu where anything that might be remotely healthy for you is fried into submission. Zucchini sticks, anybody? And while it may be fine fare for a frat party, hot wings and nachos isn't exactly the dinner of champions. So, it was a nice night ... except for the surly service.

The waitress who took our order was brusque but efficient, so I didn't think too much of it at first. The restaurant was crowded. All the servers where hustling to take orders and bring drinks and meals to their tables. A small red flag went up when the waitress dashed away without asking if we wanted any appetizers, but I really didn't need a plate of fried calamari, did I?

The food came quickly – prime rib for him, shrimp scampi for me – and it was delicious. We ate leisurely, show time still an hour away. When we were done, a bus boy came by and unobtrusively cleared the table. I hadn't seen our waitress since placing our order, but that was okay. We weren't in a rush. It was nice to sit and let our food digest.

Over the next 30 minutes the restaurant emptied out. Our waitress made the rounds to the remaining tables, laughing and smiling with the other customers. She told the table of people next to us what was for dessert: cheesecake, chocolate cake, peanut butter pie. Yum! When the diners seemed unsure, the waitress smiled — the first time I'd seen her teeth all evening — and said she'd bring them coffee while they decided.

When she turned from their table, I was ready with my dessert choice. I wanted to try the pie. I assumed she'd be stopping at our table next since it was on her way, but she didn't. She walked on by like I was Dionne Warwick. What the frak? We didn't even get the perfunctory "You folks doing okay?" or "I'll be right with you." It occurred to me that we also hadn't been treated to my all-time favorite: a server waiting until your mouth is full of food before asking you how everything is.

I'll be honest. My first thought was racism. But something about that assessment didn't feel right. I turned to my Husband and said, "I'm not imagining this, am I?"

"No," he said, stifling a chuckle. My anger, when not directed at him, makes him laugh. Nothing tickles him more than when I'm all aglow with righteous indignation. Apparently, I'm cute when I'm mad. When the waitress passed by our table again without acknowledgment, or dessert, I was done. I had The Face: lips pursed, jaw tight, and my left eyebrow arched to infinity. In my Husband's eyes I must have been absolutely gorgeous. Fearing an aneurism was eminent he clued me in.

"It's because we're the comedians," he said.

"So? What's that supposed to mean?"

"It means comics are notoriously bad tippers."

"We are?" I said.

"Well, I'm not and you're not, but most are. That's why nobody wants to wait on comics. She drew the short straw."

As the waitress made another consciously oblivious pass by our table my Husband said, "Excuse me, can you bring us the check when you get a chance?"

"Y'all are the comics, right?" We nodded. "You don't get a check."

"Oh, thanks," my Husband said. "Can we please have some coffee?"

"Sure," she said — sans smile — rolling her eyes as she walked away.

"See, I told you. She's acting that way because we're the comics."

"That's not an excuse for shabby service!" I said, my eyebrow still arched hazardously high as if to keep pace with my blood pressure.

"No, but it explains it. Waitresses work for tips and comics don't tip."

"Well, I wouldn't either for this kind of treatment."

"All it takes is one comic to mess it up," he said, pleading her case like a defense attorney.

Part of me sympathized, but seeing her be so gracious with the table right next to ours, and not to us, really pissed me off. I didn't know who angered me more: the waitress or the comics who might have screwed it up for the rest of us.

And now I was in a quandary: to tip or not to tip? I didn't want to reward bad service, which it certainly was. Nor did I want to reinforce the stereotype that comedians are bad tippers by leaving something small or nothing at all, which is what I really wanted to do.

In the end I compromised by breaking the law. I put a $20 bill on the table and wrote on both sides in small block letters for the world to see: "Not all comics are shitty tippers."

I over-tipped to make a point. It reminds me of that episode of an early 90s TV show, *A Different World,* where main character Whitley Gilbert (played by Jasmine Guy) goes into an upscale store. The saleswoman assumes she can't afford to shop there because she's Black and Whitley — one of my all-time favorite BAPs (Black American Princess) — buys out the store.

Yes, both Whit and I acted out of ego, but in my case it wasn't just about the waitress. She may be the frontline face of the restaurant, but the kitchen staff shares in the tips she earns too. Should the cooks and busboys pay for her piss-poor attitude? No more than I should have to pay for the bad tipping practices of previous comics.

And to my colleagues who may be guilty of terrible tipping I say please knock it off and show some class. If someone is serving you, TIP THEM, especially if the meal is free. I know, I know, you don't have any money, right? And the person taking and serving your order does? Waiting tables is not the gateway to wealth. No one is playing the stock market on 15% of your burger and fries. But if you can't afford to tip, then you can't afford to eat. Bring a sandwich, eat it outside, do the gig, and go home.

Need more incentive? The funny business is a funny business. Anybody can become somebody. You never know when the waitress you shortchange today will be the booker who won't take your calls tomorrow.

I love House Music.
I loved it back when it only had an apartment.

THE BUBLÉ-BIEBER BATTLE

I got the chance to be the warm-up comedian for the taping of *Michael Bublé's Christmas Special* on NBC. Pronounced *"Boo-Blay"* you may recognize his chart topper *"Haven't Met You Yet"* from his 2009 *Crazy Love* album. This Frank Sinatra-style crooner sang Christmas classics with Latin singer Thalia, country music star Kellie Pickler, and special guest ... wait for it ... Justin Bieber! Wow! That's a big get. What could go wrong? Funny you should ask.

I now truly understand why über-celebrities need security. The scantily clad, starry-eyed tweeners and teeners weren't so bad as they alternately swooned and screamed at the mere mention of You Know Who (Bieber not Lord Voldemort). I, however, was more deeply shaken by a young lady who I'll refer to as Psycho Girl and her cohorts, The Psycho Posse. This girl of maybe 16 didn't smile, nor did she blink. She was fierce and focused on all things Bieber.

Believe it or not, you know this girl. We all do. Hall & Oates sang about her in "Man Eater." Stephen King wrote about her in *Misery*. We saw her in the movie *Fatal Attraction,* or wait was it *C.H.U.D.?* Either way I was afraid, very afraid.

Psycho Girl came up to me. Well, actually I never saw her coming. She was just suddenly there in front of me, firing off questions. "Which way is Justin coming in? Is he coming in the same way as Michael? OMG, I have to see him! Is his manager here? What about his bodyguard?

Have you seen his bodyguard, Mike? He's wearing a green hoodie." I felt as though a wrong answer here was going to earn me a beat down from the Psycho Posse. I actually didn't have any answers and thankfully Psycho Girl and her crew soon veered off like a school of sharks scenting blood elsewhere.

I have no idea why she chose to ask me. If you know anything about entertainment, then you are well aware that on a TV show the warm-up comic is the lowest form of life next to the writers. Looking back, I think I made three critical mistakes. First, I looked friendly but as the warm-up comic, that's my job. Second, I stood still, an easy mistake to make and one that gave The Psychos a chance to focus on me. And third, I was holding a clipboard. A clipboard has the magical ability to convey power, knowledge, and authority. It's not quite as commanding as wearing a headset, but it's enough.

I wish I could say that was the end of it, but Psycho Girl and her Posse came back. She wasn't smiling, per se, but her demeanor was even more excited and agitated than before. She thrust her iPhone at me so I could see a picture of her — still not smiling — and the blurry profile of someone's nose. "That's him!" she said. "That's Justin!" Of course it was. "That's very nice," I said. "I'm happy for you." And I meant it. I was afraid not to mean it.

She swiped her finger across the screen and showed me a picture of her standing with her arms around a grungy, curly-haired, blond boy in a baseball cap. When I failed to show automatic recognition or the proper level of excitement, Psycho Girl said, "That's his drummer, So &

So!"

While I had the good sense to keep my gaze on the photo and not look Psycho Girl directly in the eye, I guess my blank stare was too much for her. She said, "You don't know him? You don't know any of them do you?" And by then I was too tired to be anything but honest and I said, "No. I'm sorry, Boo. I'm old as shit." And now it was her turn to look confused. That bought me the time I needed to slip away and get back to work.

When Michael Bublé finally brought Justin Bieber out on stage to sing "Mistletoe" from his Christmas album, the younglings went wild and began screaming, "We love you Justin!" Well, for some reason this was too much for the … um … mature women in the audience. They seemed to take this as a direct challenge and affront to their love and support for Mr. Bublé. They tried to drown out the Bieber babies by screaming, "We love YOU Michael!" And for a very tense moment it was an odd estrogen-fueled version of The Sharks vs. The Jets. If I had to put money on it, I'd say that the over 30s could have easily trounced the teens. (The former can run and fight in high heels. The latter are still learning how to walk in them.) I'm equally certain that Psycho Girl would not have hesitated to take them all out, Uma Thurman *Kill Bill*-style, if it meant she could get a clearer picture of Justin Bieber's nose.

You wouldn't think being a warm-up comic for a day is such a perilous job. Maybe next time I'll try it without a clipboard.

I love St. Patrick's Day. Everybody's drinking, laughing, and saying: "Today we're all Irish." Nobody ever says that during Black History Month.

THE BLACK COMIC PERSPECTIVE

I was asked to write an article about my experiences in the entertainment business as a Black comic. While flattered by the request, I'm not entirely sure I'm qualified to share my thoughts on the subject. Yes, I'm Black, I'm a comic, and I've been in the business for a while, but it's not that simple. It never is.

I started my career with the absurdly naive notion that I just wanted to be a comedian; not a Black comedian, but a funny comedian. I wanted to be myself with all the complexities that implies. Why only tell jokes from just one facet of my experience when I have so many? We all do. There's color, culture, ethnicity, nationality, religion, gender, sexual orientation, marital status, education, political stance, mental and physical health, height, weight, favorite color. Is any one of these influences more important, valid, or defining than another? I guess it depends on whom you talk to.

A comedy club manager once said to me, "Leighann, you're very funny, but can you be a little bit more Black?" He wasn't suggesting I get a tan. He was telling me he'd be more comfortable with his stereotypical image of who a Black person is, rather than who I really am. I also don't know what image of Blackness he had in mind. Perhaps I should have asked him to give me an example. It would have been interesting to see what influences shaped his expert opinion. Did he watch music videos? Had he taken a Black history class in college? Perhaps some of his best friends were Black. I wonder how many Jewish comics he suggested be more Jewish.

This happened by the way at a comedy club in New York City: the capital of the world; the crossroads of culture, where diversity is embraced, celebrated, and encouraged. As you can see, I have a healthy fantasy life. I dream. That's what artists do. I know we're not there yet as a species, but I hope someday we can be.

I thought one of the goals of the Civil Rights Movement was for African Americans to be seen as human beings. I don't see how playing to a stereotype serves that end. That's a game I'm not sure you can win. I call it the "How Black Are You?" game. It puts Blackness on a quantifiable scale and how you rate depends on which faction you're trying to appease, be it the ever vigilant "Soul Patrol" or Caucasian pop culture enthusiasts who fancy themselves on the cutting edge of cool. They judge you on how well you "keep it real," whatever that is. In this context it is subtly implied that being *Cosby Show* Black is somehow less authentic than being *Good Times* Black. Apparently, I cannot be both urban and urbane. One is somehow a betrayal of the other.

Some would say I've been foolish. Being yourself is a sweet ideal, but if I had any true business sense at all I'd see that stereotypes sell. Why not simply embrace my Blackness for creative expediency and financial gain? I don't know. Sex sells too, but I have been equally reluctant to stroll the boulevard. I don't wear my culture on my sleeve. Color really is only skin deep. These things are an important part of who I am as a person and as an artist, but again, they're not the only part.

So I'm not sure I rate high enough on the Barometer of Blackness to write this piece but I tried. As my experience with the club manager clearly demonstrates, while I see myself as a multifaceted human being, many do not or cannot. Some of these folks work in the industry. This makes my job and how I choose to do it harder and yet even more important. If all you see at the end of my show is the color of my skin, then maybe I haven't done my job right. But every time I get on stage and inspire an audience to see past the obvious, and laugh, I win. We win.

Women are 52% of the population but we only make 85 cents on the dollar. That's why I don't feel bad about shoplifting. I'm just trying to break even.

So, About the Letterman Thing

It's been an eventful time for women in comedy. The *New York Times* broke the story that female comedians are not booked to perform on the *Letterman Show* in equal numbers to their male counterparts. You don't say. Women in comedy not being treated fairly? Well gosh darn it stop the presses. This is not news to anyone with a vagina, but hats off to the *New York Times* for being in the vanguard of non-current events.

Here's the real scoop: no one in entertainment is treated fairly, least of all the talent. And that inequity is parceled out on a sliding scale: women, people of color, LGBTs, the left-handed ... I suspect that even entertainment executives feel slighted when some fem-loving reporter riles up the sponsors of their long-running successful late-night show for no reason. They're probably thinking, "Dear god, it's not even Women's Month, why is this happening?"

I will not argue that women ARE funny and would do well on ANY show. In the 21st century? Why should I bother? If you think women are funny, they're funny; if they think they're not, they're not. If you're a human adult who still thinks in absolutes then you don't deserve the opposable thumbs you were born with.

I will say that I was surprised when the talent booker for *Letterman,* was fired. I'm still not sure why. He had the job for over 10 years. If he wasn't doing exactly what Dave wanted they would have let him go a long time ago. But hey, I guess they can't fire Dave now can they? And let's be clear, the booker was only fired from one of his jobs.

He's still doing warm-up and making an annual stand-up appearance on the show. So at best he's only kinda sorta fired. That's what I call standing by your man.

What's all the brouhaha about? What did he say that riled up the women in comedy and those who laugh at us?

"There are a lot less female comics who are authentic."

"I see a lot of female comics who to please an audience will act like men."

Hmm ... having the courage to get on stage in front of an often inebriated and sometimes hostile audience, speaking our minds, wearing pants ... yeah, it doesn't get more masculine than that now does it? You know what's not masculine: The money.

He might think some inauthentic female comedians act like men to get laughs, but we certainly aren't paid like men. I've talked about the gender-pay disparity in comedy so often that I'm almost bored by it. Almost. Carping that women aren't funny is a laughable none-issue by comparison.

I recently did a gig where six comedians regardless of their gender or level of comedic authenticity were hired to do 15 minutes each. Easy breezy. The women on the show, myself included, made a $100. Not bad for a Thursday night in the city, I thought, until I learned that at least one of the men on the show made $250. In case you're wondering:

No, he did not close the show.

No, he did not have the most experience or credits.

No, he was not the advertised draw for the evening. In fact, he picked up the gig at the last minute.

And just when we thought we'd emerged from the dark ages of white male privilege.

I'm sure there are times when being a Black woman works professionally to my advantage. I'm hard pressed to say exactly when that is, though. I guess if me and a dude were going out for the same Upper West Side nanny job I'd be golden, especially if I showed up to the interview speaking in a generic Caribbean accent.

Women also earn more money in porn. Well, White women do. I'm actually not sure how Black women fare. Kinda not all that eager to find out, but if this bad economy drags on who knows? I might need to diversify.

When I began my career in comedy they said you needed to write, develop, and perform great material. Then I was told I needed good representation. Then I was told I needed solid TV credits. Well, 7,226 days later I feel like a fool for not just working on my authenticity and machismo.

Believe it or not, I'm not angry. Stop laughing. I'm not. I know that life's not fair. I know there are bigger problems on the planet. I'm not even angry with the male colleague who made 150% more than I did for the same gig. I would have taken the money and ran too if I'd had the chance.

However, if I and the other female comics on the show

were indeed trying to act like men, we should have jumped the higher paid male comic in the parking lot and taken his money. Better yet, we should have jumped the booker and taken all the money. I don't mean to imply that male comedians or bookers are thugs, just the inauthentic ones who, off-stage, act like sensitive women in order to get laid.

It's tough times for everybody. A fellow comedian recently told me that only 1% of us make a living solely as entertainers. That's a staggeringly small number and still probably an over-estimate. But if you're in the 1% it's something (in this case) to be proud of, especially if you're a woman. Doing it with a vaginal handicap makes you an authentic bad ass.

So, is it really a big deal when you don't see as many women as men in stand-up spots on late-night TV? No show is a star maker for comedians anymore, but here's what an appearance can do:

It can give you a coveted credit.

It can raise your visibility in the industry and grow your fan base.

It can, I daresay, even raise your asking price. That would be nice since I am, after all, earning less money than men for the same gigs.

It isn't just about not being on *Letterman*, it's about being effectively cock-blocked (or would that be twat-blocked?) from greater opportunities for financial gain. So yeah, it does fucking matter. I'm sorry if that last sentence seems inauthentic and masculine. But in all fairness, I wasn't trying to make you laugh.

I'm sure the former talent booker for *Letterman* is not alone in his opinions about female comedians. Insidious ideas have a way of trickling down the food chain and contributing to the notion that women are somehow less than. And if we are then don't we deserve less? Maybe even $150 less.

And yet, without a late-night TV-show credit under my man belt (I know, I'm shocked too) I'm still somehow managing to be in the 1%. Imagine where I would be if I were an authentic male stand-up comedian who was "right" for *Letterman*.

It's hard being self-employed.
I can't call in sick.
I know I'm lying.

GIMME ONE REASON TO STAY HERE

For the first time in my entire career as a professional performer, I walked out on a gig. I picked up my purse, bid farewell to the Promoter-Booker-DeeJay, and took my Black Ass home. There have been many gigs over the years that I wished I had walked out on. Or just had the flat out good sense to say no to them in the first place.

There have been:

Corporate gigs where the people are too afraid to laugh, perhaps subconsciously believing that laughers are the first to be fired.

Country club gigs, where the people are too uptight to laugh.

Bar gigs where patrons would rather watch the sporting event du jour on TV than the comedy show.

Outdoor gigs which are not always bad but are always a challenge. The good news is they offer an easy means of egress when things go as badly as the odds and your experience tells you it will.

I remember doing a show years ago in New Jersey that should've been great. It was a sold out event for a prominent women's group. What could go wrong? For starters the sound system was not working properly. It was also completely inadequate for the room of 500 chatty women who were, quite frankly, just excited to be out and away from their families. Their temporary freedom, lubricated by the open bar, was really all the entertainment they needed. The comedy show was superfluous.

As the venue tried to fix the sound system on the fly, the show stopped and re-started multiple times. This went unnoticed by the audience. They were busy scarfing down the remnants of a prime rib dinner.

There were three comics on the show that night, but that dwindled down to two when one of them turned to me and said, "I'm not doing this. I'm out of here." And then he left. Just like that. I was stunned. This was not a newbie comic who was afraid to tackle a tough room. He was a seasoned veteran who knew that stand-up comedy loses its power and allure when a comedian has to shout all of his set-ups and punch lines. Comedians don't need much, but good sound in a large room, with a big audience is definitely on the short list.

I was deeply in awe of his courage. He chose the integrity and quality of the performance he could deliver over money. But it's not just about the Benjamins. It's also about your word. If you say you'll show up and perform, people expect you to do just that. Reneging seems like a mark that goes onto your permanent record. But as I watched the other comic leave, everything inside me screamed, "Wait! Don't leave me here! Take me with you!"

But I stayed and did the show; and there was no joy in it. The audience, en-mass, was never entertained. In fact, there seemed to be a schism. A goodly number of folks had finally caught onto the idea that there was a comedy show going on, and they were trying to enjoy it. But it's hard to enjoy what you cannot hear. The ocean-wide dance floor between the crowd and me didn't help either. The other audience members seemed deeply resentful that they were being forced to endure an annoying background buzzing sound while inhaling their strawberry cheesecake.

But I stuck it out in the name of professionalism, pride, and an awareness that no gig is perfect. Much like a game of cards, you play the hand you're dealt.

I thought no more about this incident until the other night when I was confronted with my own Captain Jean Luc Picard (*Star Trek the Next Generation*) "Here and no further" moment.

And I can't tell you exactly what my tipping point was in this comedy show turned open mic. It could have been the super-sized deejay booth looming large behind the comics, making it seem like they were performing in front of the Supreme Court. Maybe it was that the Promoter-Booker-DeeJay chose to start the show even though his emcee had yet to arrive. Was it the fact that the comics on the show outnumbered the audience? This wasn't hard to do since there was only one guy there to see the show. Was it that the highlight of the opening comic's act was her sitting in the lap of said Lone Audience Member making it an awkward comedy show turned lap dance? Or maybe it was just the moment when the Promoter-Booker-DeeJay said to me with a straight face: "I don't know what happened. It was packed last week."

In any event, I was suddenly gripped with the fear that if I didn't leave soon, I may not ever be able too. I was unshakably sure that I was sitting in the comedy club equivalent of "Hotel California". ("Home by the Sea" for you Genesis fans.) And just outside of my peripheral vision Rod Serling was narrating a very special episode of the *Twilight Zone* just for me.

This wasn't a matter of money (I wasn't getting any) or pride (clearly, taking this gig, I didn't have any). But I now knew that not every show should be done. There was nothing I could accomplish and indeed I might be doing damage that my therapist would not have the skill to undo.

And so I left.

As Gloria Gaynor bid her errant lover do, I walked out the door. A part of me wanted to feel bad about this, but I only felt liberated. I imagine it was how Kunta Kinte might have felt if he had actually managed to get away, foot intact. In the end I know I made the right decision. Sometimes it takes as much courage to leave as it does to stay.

I gave money to a homeless man.
He said, "Thank you Miss. Get home safe."
I said, "You're welcome, you too... oh."

Very Funny Bag Lady?

So, I ran into a fellow comedian whom I love and respect a great deal. He's one of those guys who is the cherished combination of funny and nice. I've always admired his success. I've seen him in commercials, he's a respected regular in the A-level comedy clubs around the city, and he had his own Comedy Central special. Since I hadn't seen him in a while I had assumed he was doing his thing out in Los Angeles. So I was crushed when he told me he's now selling real estate.

How in the hell do you go from Comedy Central to Century 21?

My Friend said he was tired: tired of the road, tired of beating his head against the wall of the entertainment industry. "I did everything," he said, "I auditioned, wrote scripts, took pitch meetings — but I just don't know what they want." And now I'm scared, because apparently I don't know what they want either.

Part of me admires that My Friend could look at his life so objectively and say, "What do I want the next 20 years to be?" And then do something pro-active and positive for his financial and professional future. He, of course, still does shows from time to time. Essentially, leaving the business put him in a better position to say "no" to the crappy gigs he doesn't want. But on the other hand, how do you let go of a dream? It's hard to see someone who's so talented, someone who I thought had a shot, throw in the towel and say, "I'm done."

I don't know if I can do that, leave Stand-Up. I don't know how to do anything else. No, that's not true. I don't want to do anything else. I never have. Most people are afraid to get on stage and tell jokes. I'm afraid not to.

But now I'm also afraid I'll be the comedic equivalent of one of those old jazz musicians that only other old jazz musicians know, and the public never heard of. I'm afraid I'll pass unnoticed by the people in the industry who could make a real difference in my career because I don't fit into their predetermined little boxes and so they don't know what to do with me.

I heard that George Lopez was on the verge of quitting comedy when Sandra Bullock saw him, loved him, got behind him, and helped him get his TV show. Where's my Sandra?

You see, Stand-Up and I had an agreement. If I gave it my time, my energy, and my all, if I, as Ntozake Shange wrote in *For Colored Girls,* "loved it assiduously," it would bring me things in return. Little things like fame and fortune.

I've given up a lot for Stand-Up. I watched my friends have normal lives, regular jobs, houses, kids, and really weird stuff like retirement plans and health insurance. My Husband once said to me that he knew I loved Stand-Up more than I loved him. I wanted to say he was wrong, but the look in his eyes told me not to even try to tell that lie, and the feeling in my heart of hearts agreed.

Our first big fight as a married couple was over Stand-Up. I was invited to go to the Middle East to perform for the troops and I accepted without even running it by him. To be honest, it never even occurred to me. Why would it? It's Stand-Up.

My biggest fear is that I've been a fool. Entertainment is not a guaranteed return on investment. And as I get older I have to wonder, like My Friend, can I put in another 20 years? And what if the answer is no? If I don't get out now, will I just end up being a very funny bag lady?

But I don't want to sell real estate.

I love Stand-Up but I don't know any more if it loves me back. I don't know if it ever did. I'd always assumed that I would never leave Stand-Up. But the bigger, ever more pressing question is: if I did leave, would it even notice that I was gone? Or would it just assume that I was just doing my thing out in Los Angeles?

TRUE STORY

I carry a big handbag. Whatever you need, I got it.
Need a pen? I got it. Piece of gum? I got it.
Sham Wow? Don't ask questions. Just know I got it.

THE PRICE OF PRIVY PRIVACY

I walked into the bathroom and there she was: a woman dressed in black pants, dark-patterned vest, and a crisp white shirt. I'd never met her before but I knew her. She was The Bathroom Attendant. It had been a while since I'd seen one. This is probably more of a commentary on the caliber of the establishments I frequent then on how many attendants there might be in the city. A typical haunt for me can be lovingly described as a hole in the wall, where the services of an attendant are unnecessary, unless she is also a plumber.

Bathroom Attendants appear mostly in the facilities of upscale establishments. They are supposed to bespeak an atmosphere of luxury and personal service offering users soap, towels, lotion, deodorant, gum, condoms; but it might be time to get off the merry go round if The Bathroom Attendant is a integral part of your safe sex plans.

The Bathroom Attendant is as outdated as The Elevator Operator. The latter hails from a time when elevators qualified as heavy machinery. You couldn't have the general public opening and closing their own elevator doors and pushing their own buttons could you? That would be madness. I imagine the job of The Bathroom Attendant was similarly created to guide people through those heady days when indoor plumbing was fresh and new. "How do I flush this thing? Where do I wash my hands? What can I dry them with? Somebody help me!" Bathroom Attendant to the rescue!

But now we push our own buttons and flush our own toilets. The Bathroom Attendant has not only become unnecessary, but an intrusion. It feels particularly invasive when the bathroom is not crowded. When it's just me and her. I feel so judged.

When I'm safely locked behind my stall door, I wonder what she's doing. Is she listening? How can she not? For giggles, does she carry a stopwatch to time how long visitors urinate? If so, how do I rate? Suddenly I'm in competition with past pee-ers.

And what if I'm engaged in more... um ... personal work? Oh god, is she listening then too? How could she not? Given my druthers, I'd prefer a little privacy; keeping whatever gastrointestinal difficulties I may or may not be having to myself. I'd rather not be identified as the Chick with the Cranky Colon in stall number three.

And then there's the matter of the tip. Do you or do you not? There are three reasons to tip: the first is for services rendered. I'm all up for living in the lap of luxury, truly I am. But I can pump out my own soap and reach for my own paper towel. Anything else the attendant can offer, I've already got in my mammoth handbag: lotion, nail file, perfume, safety pins... I'm my own attendant. The second reason to tip is guilt. What you give them is probably all they're making. But why should I pay for a service I neither need nor want? Nonetheless I do feel bad not giving The Bathroom Attendant something. But it's the kind of guilt I can live with.

And then there's the apology tip. When I've been in there by myself behind my locked door, and she on the other side with her stopwatch, I give her the "I'm sorry you had to hear that" tip. How can I not? I put a dollar in her cup and wish I could have tipped her not to be there in the first place. Privacy. That's the real luxury worth paying for.

A thousand years from now, what are archaeologists going to say about us when they start digging up Starbucks? "We believe this is where they worshipped."

Caramel Macchiato, Now with Extra TMI

I walked into my local Starbucks and there was a man who had transformed an entire section into his own personal corner office. He had several tables and chairs arrayed around him topped with books and papers. Every available outlet in his vicinity had been commandeered to power a seemingly endless number of his gadgets: laptop, cell phone, iPod, a portable printer. I'm not sure, but I think I saw a humidifier. If there were an electrical fire, he would have been the first to go.

Corner Office Guy looked so relaxed and comfortable I felt as though I was invading his space. I was reluctant to sit down anywhere near him but then I remember I had overpaid to be there, too. I don't complain about the price of coffee at Starbucks because that's not all I'm there for. When I just want coffee, I go to Dunkin Donuts. When I want ambiance I go to Starbucks. It has comfy chairs, good service, nice music, and an air of safety and serenity. It's not just a coffee shop. It's temporary office space, within limits.

With his face illuminated by the glow of his super-sized laptop, and a blue tooth ear piece plugged into the side of his head, Corner Office Guy looked like he was all about taking care of business, but looks can be deceiving. I soon realized why the seat closest to him was open and available. He was talking on his cell phone using his outdoor voice. Cell phones have obliterated the line between convenience and courtesy. Just because you can have a conversation anywhere doesn't mean you should. I wish they'd bring back phone booths.

I don't think I would have minded if he were on the phone wheeling and dealing. If he had been negotiating a low interest rate on a business loan or tracking down a missed FedEx delivery. I would have respected that. But the intimate details he revealed in what should have been a private conversation transformed him from Corner Office Guy to Too Much Information (TMI) Guy.

He regaled everyone in Starbucks with a story about a recent sexual affair he'd had with a married woman in the Hamptons. They "saw" each other no less than four times a week. Things were fine until her husband got suspicious and decided to test her fidelity by insisting that she – his wife - sleep with him. She did. And this was too much for TMI Guy. As he explained to his friend on the phone (and to all of us in Starbucks) he had to break up with her. He simply couldn't stand the idea of his girlfriend sleeping with her husband.

Why do I know this? I shouldn't know this. Don't Ask, Don't Tell has its place. And that place is Starbucks. If we bring back phone booths we should also seriously consider bringing with it the other things so severely lacking in our culture like boundaries, discretion, and good judgment.

I expect this kind of shenanigans at Dunkin Donuts. But Starbucks has standards, an unspoken code of conduct. I don't expect us all to sip our lattes in silence. But if we're going to spend a few hours together in our temporary office space, we should at least agree to use our indoor voices, share the electrical outlets, and not inflict ourselves on each other. Starbucks might start charging for coffee and the show.

Oddly enough I went to Starbucks to write a new blog post but I don't remember what it was going to be about because TMI Guy's story took its place.

You're not a size zero if people can see you.

ZUMBA BY ANY MEANS NECESSARY

When I first heard about Zumba I didn't pay it any mind because I wasn't interested in another exercise fad. Remember when hot yoga was hot? Pilates? Pul-lease. I'm embarrassed now to think of how much I weakened my living room floorboards by trying to keep up with my Billy Blanks Tae Bo tapes. But when I got an opportunity to take a free Zumba class I figured why not.

This winter has not been my friend. Severe low temperatures and back-to-back snowstorms did not inspire me to go to the gym. Add in all my broken promises to excavate my exercise mat from behind the couch and work out at home, and its no surprise that my hips are looking hippier than I'd like. To paraphrase Beyoncé, I don't think you're ready for this belly.

Zumba, according to my friends at Wikipedia, is "a brand name for a fitness program consisting of dance and aerobic exercise routines performed to popular, mainly Latin-American music." That sounded promising since I love to dance. No, I mean: LOVE to dance. And it turns out that I enjoy Zumba so much that I'm sorry I didn't try it sooner. It was just as much fun as partying at a nightclub but without the cover charge, over-priced drinks, and high heel shoes.

I guess it all starts with The Instructor. She's very encouraging and all are welcome so there's a wide range of skill levels. There are women who look like they're perfecting their strip-club pole skills while there are others who completely destroy the stereotype that all Black people have rhythm. And that's okay. We aren't auditioning for Alvin Ailey. We're there to have fun and work out to the best of our ability.

It's particularly inspiring to see the older women in class who are not letting their age diminish their vibrancy. But I'll be honest there are a couple of them who scare me. We forget sometimes – or maybe it's just me – that an older woman was once a young woman. And I've seen these current nanas (former ill nanas) work it like they can still put a hurtin' on a man. They may not be flat out dropping it like it's hot, but they can still wave it like it's warm.

Now, you would think a gymnasium of 50 plus women (I think men are allergic to Zumba) would begin to smell a little rank. But once we get going, this group of Black women smells like a beautiful blend of baby powder and Carol's Daughter body lotion.

The most awkward part of the class is seeing the portraits of dead Civil Rights leaders that adorn the walls. If you haven't guessed, this free class is offered in my neighborhood and I live in The Hood. I feel a little self-conscious shaking what my momma gave me under the grave, bespectacled gaze of Malcolm X. But I think he would approve of me getting in shape by any means necessary.

Babies will instinctively dance when they hear music, and smile more when they are on time with the beat. And then somewhere along the line, for some melanin-deprived males, things go horribly, horribly wrong.

ROB BASE IS NOT DEAD

Rob Base is not dead. But I thought he was. Here's what happened. After doing a joke about old-school rap, an audience member came up to me after the show and said, "Did you know that Rob Base died?" What? I was flabbergasted. "Joy & Pain" Rob Base? "It Takes Two Rob Base?" No. I didn't know. To be honest I really haven't been right since we lost Heavy D.

She told me that Rob had presumably been murdered and his car – a 1998 minivan – had been stolen. As we commiserated over the sad news, it bothered her deeply that Rob Base died living such an ordinary life. It doesn't get any more ordinary than a minivan. There is an illusion that once famous, always famous; once successful, always successful; once wealthy, always wealthy. Even if you're not in the public eye, day walkers (non-entertainers) like to assume that you're off somewhere being famous and fabulous. Sadly, no.

What bothered both of us was that the death of Rob Base was not front-page news. He deserved better than that. I should've turned on CNN and heard it straight from Anderson Cooper's mouth. My Mom contends that if you ever want to get news about Black celebrities, you have to read *Jet Magazine*. You'll get the news late, but you'll get it.

On the drive home I began to wonder how the mainstream media could have dropped the ball so badly on the death of a Hip-Hop icon. That's when I remembered that I have a degree in journalism and every now and then one must verify a story. Just because you're dead on the

Internet doesn't mean you're dead for real. You go a weekend without a status update and folks can get a little nervous.

Once, on a ferry ride to a gig on Fire Island, one of my fellow comics pointed to a handsome older gentleman and whispered: "Oh my god! That's Mike D'Amato. He played for the NY Jets and won the '68 super bowl." The other comic said, "No, he won it in '67." Not one to live with ambiguity when I don't have to, I checked and according to Google, Mike D'Amato won the Super Bowl in 1968. But Google also said Mike D'Amato was dead. Now, if I thought he looked good for an old guy, then he looked absolutely fantastic for a dead guy. The first comic said, "Aww man, do you think he'd mind if I asked him for his autograph?" I said, "I don't know. Do zombies give autographs?"

It turns out, of course, that Rob Base is not dead either. Chandler Spencer is. Who's Chandler Spencer? He's the guy who sang the background R&B hook to *Joy & Pain*. While sad, I can see why the mainstream media might have missed it. Lots of people die under the radar. I didn't find out until months after the fact that Blossom Deary had died. Who's Blossom Deary? That depends on what generation you're from. If you're from my parents' generation, Blossom Dearie was the diminutive pianist and jazz singer with the girlish voice. If you're from my generation, then she was the voice behind one of your favorite *School House Rock* songs: "Unpack my Adjectives." Yeah, *that's* Blossom Dearie.

I had the pleasure of seeing her perform live at Danny's

Skylight Lounge in NYC, before she died … naturally. Tupac Shakur hologram aside, dead people don't normally do concerts. I was delighted to hear her sing about things other than parts of speech. My favorite was Blossom's Blues:

> *My name is, Blossom*
> *I was raised in the lions' den.*
> *My name is, Blossom*
> *I was raised in the lions' den.*
> *My nightly occupation?*
> *Stealing other women's men.*

> *I'm an evil, evil woman*
> *But I want to do a man some good.*
> *I'm evil, evil woman*
> *But I want to do a man some good.*
> *I'm Gina Lollobrigida*
> *I ain't red riding hood.*

> *If you don't like my peaches, baby*
> *Why do you shake my tree?*
> *If you don't like my peaches, baby*
> *Why do you shake my tree?*
> *Stay out of my orchard, baby*
> *Let my peach tree be.*

What do Rob Base and Blossom Dearie have in common? Me. I'm probably the only person on the planet who digs them both. So I'm glad that Rob Base is okay. I am sorry about Chandler Spencer and my condolences go out to his family. I more than a little bit wish that the Overweight Lover was still in the house. And it makes me worry. Has anybody seen Grandmaster Flash lately? At the very least, it might be time for him to get his prostate checked.

If Bill Gates were a country, he would be the 37th richest country on Earth. If I were a country, the Red Cross would airlift me food.

A BEAUTIFUL DAY FOR A PROTEST

Two friends invited me to go with them to the Occupy Wall Street protest in New York City and I said yes for selfish reasons. First, I hoped to get a good story out of it. Second, the weather forecast predicted 80 degrees and sunny. What better conditions to exercise my constitutional rights? Yes, I'm a fair-weather protester. I don't work for the United States Post Office. If the forecast had been for inclement weather, the only protesting I would have done would have been from behind my keyboard at a Starbucks.

And while I never considered going to Occupy alone, I was more than happy to go in a group. Friends don't let friends demonstrate alone. I guess that literally makes me a social activist. The Unabomber went solo and look what happened to him. For starters, a horrible mug shot.

After deciding to go to the protest the next big decision was what to wear. I mean, really, what do you wear to an occupation? There are protests in the Middle East all the time, but they don't show a lot of women, and the men are all wearing facial hair and anger.

I guess, very practically, you should put on something you wouldn't mind wearing to jail. I wasn't planning on going, but I had to at least consider the possibility. I'm brown. Brown people go to jail more frequently, for fewer reasons and for longer periods of time than do non-brown people. It's like some kind of hyper-regressive form of Affirmative Action. I settled on black jeans and a t-shirt that read, "I Was in Paris." It was both an homage to the French

Revolution and a possible alibi.

I also needed a plan. I considered the direct approach: introducing myself to the officer in charge and saying, "Excuse me, Sir? Where do I need to stand, how do I need to act, and what do I need to do in order to not get your attention?" Plan "B" was standing next to someone browner than me.

I was also a bit concerned about the possibility of physical violence. The images of people being pepper sprayed by the police for no reason are chilling. Should I consider adding safety goggles to my ensemble? I was also worried that by the time I got to the protest the police would have stepped up their game from pepper spraying to tasering. Low-level electrocution can be hell on a hair do, which reminded me to bring a hat.

And as a general rule of thumb, you never want to be the first person tased. Everyone's excited and pumped-up. The combined jolt of electricity and the adrenaline could kill you. And any money that comes from the resulting lawsuit wouldn't benefit you. It would be posthumously awarded to your family. Bummer.

So, my reasons for going to the Occupy Wall Street protest were mostly shallow, but not completely. I do agree with what the demonstration stands for. If you don't know, I recommend you visit http://occupywallst.org/ Let's face it, you're not really a movement until you have a website. In a nutshell, they are demonstrating against the growing wealth inequality and the corporate influence of government.

The American Dream has been stolen from the world. Workers are told that they aren't allowed health care, shelter, food. Students are told that they aren't allowed jobs, and that they will be in debt for the rest of their lives, unable to declare bankruptcy. The 1% has destroyed this nation and its values through their greed. The 1% has stolen this world. We will not allow this to occur.

Hell yeah! What they said.

Occupy movements are spreading to other cities across the United States and Canada. I have no idea why the Canadians are protesting. Perhaps it's their proximity to a rapidly declining world power that threatens to suck them down with it.

There are, of course, those who are speaking out against Occupy Wall Street, denouncing it as anti-capitalist. Seriously? I mean, really, what would that counter protest look like? People in suits shouting greed is good; poor people suck?

Ironically, had my life gone according to plan, I might have been one of the people the Occupy Wall Street folks were protesting against. In college I started out as a finance major. Judge me if you must, but I was young and I wanted to be Alex P. Keaton. My plan was to work on Wall Street, to be a broker in the pit, wheeling and dealing with the big boys. That's right, if I had only stayed the course I, too, could have played a part in bringing down the world economy and destroying people's lives.

I'm glad I didn't. The one percent might've made me their fall girl. Perhaps convicted on a charge of economic terrorism I would have been the one to go to jail. Because you know it's the brown ones always do.

Global warming is real.
I've had turtlenecks and shorts in the same load of laundry.

HELLRAISER

"Leighann," he said, "What's your favorite romantic movie?" Believe it or not I've never been asked that before so I had to think about it for a second. My head tilted to the left, my eyes stared off into space, and my body went still. I do that sometimes when completely caught off guard. It looks like I'm processing a data download from My Mothership. "What's my favorite romantic movie?" I was as shocked as anyone when I heard myself say, *Hellraiser.*

Um... what?

To the best of my conscious knowledge *Hellraiser* has never been classified as a romantic movie by anyone, ever. It's not even my favorite film. It's actually one of the few horror flicks that truly scare me. For years I couldn't even watch it. Years! But it wasn't Pin Head who put me off. I grew up in New York City. A guy with needles sticking out of his head in a perfect grid pattern isn't scary. That's a creative casual Friday.

The Puzzle Box terrified me. I never learned how to solve puzzles as a kid and the longer we don't understand something the scarier we allow it become. The Rubik's Cube my parents gave me only served to exacerbate my feelings of mental inadequacy. Yeah, I'm sure there's a trick to solving it, but I never got the email. And so I was happy when the Rubik's Cube crazy faded from pop culture prominence and very relieved that my admission to college didn't depend on solving it. I'm okay with The Cube being a multicolored paperweight.

Yet, it still intrigued me that my subconscious served up *Hellraiser* as a romantic movie. Was it going for the joke as my conscious mind often does? Maybe; maybe not. Perhaps my subconscious knows me better than I give it credit for. On the surface, *Hellraiser* is not a romantic movie. But it's so much easier and fun to watch while wrapped up in the arms of that someone special where I can easily hide my face away from the scary bits in the crook of their shoulder. And that, my friends is romantic. Assuming said armpit of love is clean and deodorized.

But slightly more worrying than saying *Hellraiser* is my favorite romantic movie is that The Mother Ship and I still have yet to think of a better answer.

I tried to flip my mattress. It might have been easier to flip a house. If you need me I'll be at the chiropractor.

I Fell Out of Bed

Have you ever had one of those days? Mine started the night before last when I fell out of bed. I wish I could say I was doing something fun when it happened. I was simply sitting crossed-legged on the edge and leaning over to plug in my phone. I overextended just a little and gravity made me regret not springing for thicker carpet.

I didn't have far to fall and it happened fast. I only had time to say "Woooo!" and it was over. But in that surreal, slow motion way that's depicted so well in the movies I had time to think:

Oh no!

I'm not falling am I?

Is this really happening?

Oh crap! This is really happening!

My grown, black ass is falling out of bed!

Oh, this is some shameful shit!

Of course, I landed with my legs still underneath me so my knees, calves, and the tops of my feet took the brunt of the fall. The impact was loud but it didn't wake anyone but my Dog who seemed supremely annoyed that I'd disturbed him. He looked at me as if to say, "You know, this wouldn't happen if you just slept on the floor like I do." Then he got up and walked away. He didn't even have the decency to come over and sniff me to see if I was okay.

I unfolded myself and assessed the damage. Although my left foot really hurt, my bruised but still intact Vanity wondered, "Will I be able to wear those new boots I bought?" Priorities people. Priorities.

The next morning I hobbled out of bed – lots of errands to run – but not 30 seconds into the drive I heard a horrible grinding sound coming from the right side of my car. That sound said:

This is not good.

This is going to be expensive.

This is going to cut into your boot budget.

On the bright side, I wasn't far from my local mechanic. He heard me coming from down the block. As I pulled into the station he said, *"I guess you want me to check that out."* I tried my best to follow along when he told me everything that was wrong. All I really heard was, "Right, front brake … hose … caliper … parts and labor … $300. You want me to fix it?" I just nodded my head. I didn't have a lot of options. I couldn't drive around sounding like killer whales on a mating spree. And in a way, I counted myself lucky. Had I taken my car to the dealership my bill would easily have been double.

An hour and a half later, I was back on the road, Dog in tow, heading to the vet. My Dog had given us a big scare. He was vomiting, not eating, and the Vet's X-ray looked bad enough to warrant a sonogram. (This might explain His Lordship's surliness when I'd interrupted his sleep with my inconsiderate fall.) We feared cancer but thankfully, extra tests ruled that out. However, on top of having dry skin, a bad thyroid, arthritis, and glaucoma, my Dog is now ... wait for it ... anemic.

My Vet said the best thing for anemia is liver. Not liver treats, not liver snacks. Real liver. And we then had a five-minute conversation on the best way to shop for, prepare, and cook liver for my Dog. Too bad I'd already spent most of my liver money at the Mechanic.

So, at the end of the day, car fixed, old Dog reasonably healthy but still old, I settled in for a very sexy evening of doing laundry. No sarcasm here. I often find joy in the little things like clean clothes.

I was on my second load of laundry when I noticed the water on the floor. Yes, my washing machine was now leaking. I've got a call out to the Maytag Repair Man and I'm hoping it's just a hose and I don't need a brand new machine. I don't want to dip in on the money I've ear marked for liver. But the way things are going, a new machine may indeed be in the offing.

When my head started to throb in time with my left foot — the one I'd fallen on less than 24 hours ago — I realized I hadn't eaten anything all day. A simple bowl of cereal would suffice. Thankfully I had a full container of milk in the fridge. Too bad it had expired three weeks ago.

Son of a bitch!

I was going to throw the milk away but it occurred to me that I might now be destroying an entire civilization. And maybe that's how we got started. If there's such a thing as a god, maybe He/She/It/All of the Above was having one of those days and never got around to throwing the milk away. You know: The Milk Creation Myth. Hmm, maybe when I fell out of bed I hit my head as well.

The next day, this gave me a lot to talk about with my therapist. She was nice enough to give me a little extra time in our session. But more time with her meant not enough time on the meter and now I have a shiny new $115 parking ticket that's cutting into my Boot, Car, Liver, and Washing Machine Budget.

Voltaire once said, "Any fool can survive a crisis. It's the day-to-day living that wears you out." Preach, it Volti!

Tonight if I fall out of bed again I'm just going to lay there and think about returning my boots, sharing my Dog's liver, traveling by public transportation, and using more Febreeze until I get my washing machine fixed. And maybe, whatever is evolving in my milk container will worship me as its all-powerful, sexy-boot wearing, hard-driving, dog-owning, mother goddess, and take up a second collection for my new washer-dryer.

Yeah. I definitely hit my head.

Women who play video games tend to have more sex and be happier with their relationships than those who don't. If anyone needs me, I'll be at the arcade.

GAME NIGHT - A NOT SO TRIVIAL PURSUIT

A close friend recently hosted a Game Night and all of us who attended were charged with bringing our favorites. Rising to the challenge, I brought a goodie bag full of Old School: dominoes, cloth and wire jump ropes for Double Dutch, and a sack full of classic metal jacks. You heard me. Jacks! Yeah, I took it there. You can't get metal jacks anymore. You see, now we care about children choking on small metal objects, in my generation not so much. I'm not saying parents back in day ate their young, but they didn't see the need to overprotect us from toys made with lead, asbestos, mercury, or depleted uranium.

When I sprinkled my biohazard jacks out of their black suede pouch, my comrades "Oooed" and "Ahhhed" like I had just whipped out a handful of non-conflict diamonds. When the original hard, high-bounce balls tumbled out too, the consensus was I could probably get a bundle for them from the guys on *Pawn Stars*. (We checked and learned that except for the memories, my jacks are worthless.)

One day when I was about 11-years-old, friends of my Mom's saw me playing jacks and asked to join in. I said, yes, because I was happy that adults wanted to play with me, but I was also thinking, "What do these 'old' ladies know about playing jacks?" Well, these superannuated sisters got down on their haunches and with breathtaking hand-eye coordination proceeded to wipe the floor with me. It was like the familiar scene in a pool hustler movie where The Mark lets The Ringer shoot first and then spends the rest of the game watching them literally call every shot. If we had been playing for money, I'd still be paying them off.

The Ladies – who were ancient only in the eyes of an adolescent – had to change positions more frequently than I did to accommodate older hips and knee joints, but any aches and pains they might have felt were eclipsed by the fun they were having. They laughed and trash-talked like the girls, rumor had it, they used to be:

"C'mon! You know you touched that jack!"

"No, I didn't!"

There were no husbands, kids, or jobs. They were all skill and concentration handily making it up to their tensies and back.

When I was a kid, I spent hours on my Parent's kitchen floor playing jacks. But now that my friends and I are grown with homes of our own, I knew we were hardly thinking about putting scratches on our own floors. So, in my Bag of Old School I also had a deck of Uno cards, Dominoes, Monopoly, and Trivial Pursuit. That's right, son. I'm an OG Gamer. In addition to my original, friends had brought the 80s and pop culture versions of Trivial Pursuit as well.

The night was young, the wine was good, and we were feeling groovy. "Trivial Pursuit it is!" we agreed. But we soon realized why this game has declined in popularity. It tells you things about yourself that you may not want to know. Since graduation, I've been laboring under the delusion that I am a smart woman. No. Apparently, I'm a dumb ass.

After playing Trivial Pursuit for 45 minutes I wanted to remove my college degree from the wall, return it to the Bursar's office, and get my money back. After playing for two hours, I was afraid my alma mater was going to come and take it back. As the evening progressed I became convinced that I'd go home and find an empty spot on the wall where my degree used to be, a sticky note in its place saying: "You disgust us."

I don't know how we got here. The game had started out with such promise:

Question: "In which war did the most Americans die?"

Answer: "The Civil War."

Yeah, baby! I knew the answer to that. You know why? Because that wasn't my question. One of my questions was:

"Who was the first African American to coach a major league sports team?"

I'll give you a hint. It's not Ernie Hudson. No, I didn't really think the Black guy from *Ghost Busters* was also a major league coach, but I was grasping at straws since the answer also wasn't Denzel Washington in *Remember the Titans*. For the record the answer is Bill Russell. (Mr. Russell, if you're reading this, I'm very sorry. I should have known that.)

Question: "What two numbers are evenly divisible into 17?"

Answer: "Ernie Hudson?"

"No? Oh my god, who's writing these questions? Stephen Hawking?"

But in Trivial Pursuit you're not allowed to answer a question with a question. You're also not allowed to use a lifeline, phone a friend, or surreptitiously use your smart phone to lookup the answers on Wikipedia. Ridiculous, right? As an English major I was regretting not taking my math classes more seriously.

I'd like to say that the wine impaired my intellectual faculties. But it was probably the lead from my vintage metal jacks still lingering in my system. Apparently, my childhood had a half-life. I bet if I ever get cocky enough to play Trivial Pursuit again, my question will be: "Who's the Black guy from *Ghost Busters*?" And I'll say, "Bill Russell?"

Next game night, floor damage be damned, I'm playing jacks.

Everything in the bathroom is so automated,
I'm afraid we're raising a generation of children who are
bathroom illiterate. Someday my kid might say,
"Mommy? You had to flush your own toilet?"
"And wipe my own ass, Boo. It was horrible."

Peeing Standing Up

I was lucky. While my Dad worked, my Mom stayed home with me until I was four-years-old. And then my luck ran out. Somebody got the bright idea that I needed to be "socialized" with other kids my own age and off I went to day-care. I remember there being a lot of teasing, hitting, and crying. All I wanted to do was go back home and lock myself in my room. Things haven't changed much.

I was supposed to learn how make friends and share. But if human history is an accurate measure these lessons are the hardest to learn and the easiest to forget.

Budding germaphobe that I was I disliked holding hands with the other kids, which the teachers commanded us to do all the time. *"Okay, kids. We're going to the park. Everybody hold hands."* Do I have to? Even seeing a kid wash his hands didn't cleanse away the image of him treating the inside of his nose like it was a scratch-off lottery ticket.

Of particular vexation to my young sense and sensibility was the classroom's communal bathroom, which featured two stalls with no doors. Egads, people! No doors! I guess they figured four-year olds had no right to privacy. Everyone could see what everyone else was doing and over time I couldn't help but notice that the boys sometimes went to the bathroom standing up.

I'd never seen that before because in my house our bathroom had a door and we used it. Nonetheless I was intrigued. How great would it be if I could go the bathroom with my pants up and my back to the door?

Forget friendship and sharing, why hadn't anyone taught me how to do that? We were, of course, learning new things every day, and maybe they just hadn't gotten around to it yet, but this was important. So I took matters into my own hands, no pun intended, and gave it a whirl on my own.

My intention was in the right place but biology and physics were not. Challenges quickly presented themselves. I soon realized that when the boys had their backs to me I couldn't see what they were actually doing. I knew their pants were open and that urine was hitting the water but I didn't know exactly how to make that happen. It never occurred to me that we had different standard operating equipment.

As my hoped-for stream turned into a flood, I improvised. I figured if I leaned back far enough I could achieve the proper angle and aim. But practically none of my urine made it into the bowl. It was, instead, all over my clothes.

When my teacher came in to see what was taking me so long — the non-existent door giving her a perfect view of my dangerously arched back and the puddle of pee on the floor — she said: "Leighann! What are you doing?"

"Peeing!" I said.

"You can't pee standing up!"

"No, not yet," I said over my shoulder. "But maybe with a little practice."

She said, "You've wet yourself! Do you have a change of

clothes in your cubby?"

"I did not wet myself!" You see, that implied I was a baby and that I didn't have any control. On the contrary, I was peeing with purpose. It just wasn't working out. And no, I didn't have a change of clothes hanging out in my cubby because I was four-years-old. I was a big girl and big girls don't wet themselves. My teacher brought me over to my Mom who worked in the classroom right across the hall. "Mrs. Lord," she said, "I'm sorry. Do you have a change of clothes for your daughter? She wet herself."

"I did not wet myself!" Why wasn't anybody listening? And, more importantly, why wasn't anybody teaching me how to pee standing up? My Mom, sensing there was more to the story, looked at me and said: "Okay, what happened?"

Finally! I explained and when they got the gist, it wasn't that they didn't want to laugh in my face. They were just too stunned to do it. Clothes were found. I cleaned up and changed. I spent the rest of the day in some other kid's shorts and tee shirt brooding over where my experiment had gone wrong.

News got around quickly that I'd wet myself despite my ardent explanations to the contrary. My classmates — nose pickers, butt diggers, and dirt eaters all — did not care. For the next two days I was just The Girl Who Wet Herself. Why I'd done it was completely irrelevant. On the bright side, no one wanted to hold my hand.

UNDER THE INFLUENCE

"Being funny is a wonderful thing. Lots of people are funny. But to do it at a place and time of another person's choosing, on demand, for money... that's not for everybody. That job requires a professional." - Robert Klein

GOOD NIGHT, HARVEY

Like most of America I came to know Harvey Korman from his weekly role on *The Carol Burnett Show*. I'd like to say he was my favorite cast member, but in truth I loved the whole ensemble. Each uniquely talented, the group chemistry was magical. The sketches were hilarious, and they were even better when the cast broke down and struggled not to laugh through a scene. It looked like Carol, Harvey, Tim Conway, Vicki Lawrence, and Lyle Wagner were having the time of their lives. A job with funny and talented co-workers, who make people laugh, and enjoy themselves in the process? Sign me up.

I got a chance to meet Harvey Korman in 1993 on the set of *Radioland Murders*. It was my first movie and to say I was excited is an understatement. Not knowing or caring about the Hollywood caste system I talked to everybody from the property master to the key grips and was constantly under foot. One of the highlights of this experience was chatting with Harvey Korman.

As The Old Guy on the set he was delightfully crotchety. He grumbled about the business, *Herbie the Love Bug,* and his agent. *"I've got to stop taking his calls,"* Harvey said. According to him, his agent had to talk him into doing *Radioland* when all he wanted to do was stay home. I loved every minute of it and I wasn't fooled. When the cameras started rolling, Harvey was a pure pro: in character with impeccable timing, he delivered the funny in every single take.

When he found out I was a comedian he told me to let

him know when I would be in LA because he knew the owners of The Comedy Store. I did not take him up on the offer. Though young in the business, it hadn't taken long to figure out that the phrase "look me up" is in the same league as "let's do lunch," "the check is in the mail," and "you were great!"

Cynical? Bad Hollywood stereotype? Maybe, but my experience tells me different. I've worked with more than one well-known celebrity (don't ask me, I'm not telling) who asked me to call them, their Lawyer-Agent-Manager-Flunky so we could meet-talk-have coffee-work together. How many messages do you leave before it becomes stalking?

I'm not pushy and I'm not the groupie type who gloms onto the rich and famous in the hopes that they'll do something for my career. If you dig me and want to help, that's cool. If you don't, that's fine too. Like I said, I'm not pushy; which makes unsolicited and later unrealized offers of help even more perplexing.

Maybe I'd have a better understanding of this behavior if my degree were in psychology. In lieu of enlightenment I've learned that some offers just can't be taken at face value. Sometimes — without malice — empty offers and hollow praise can drop as automatically from the tongue as does a "god bless you" to a sneeze. Sometimes a "call me" means, "don't."

Is it possible that Harvey really meant it? Absolutely, but part of me didn't want to find out if another one of my comedy idols was full of shit. The older you grow, the fewer illusions you get to keep; and you don't always get to choose which ones turn to dust. I chose to keep my happy memories of a very funny man who I was incredibly lucky to work with; who with a phone call wouldn't hesitate get me some coveted LA stage time should I need it.

For the record, if he had said he had friends at *The Tonight Show* this might have been a different story. Illusions be damned! I would've risked a restraining order for that opportunity.

There was a time when a college degree guaranteed job security. Now, Job Security are the people who escort you out of the building after you've been laid off.

IT'S ALL DENNIS MILLER'S FAULT

"A good rule of thumb is if you've made it to thirty-five and your job still requires you to wear a name tag, you've made a serious vocational error." - Dennis Miller

When I first heard this joke, I howled. I loved it. Although it smacked of elitism I still found it to be a flat-out funny line. So imagine my horror when a cruise line I do shows for asked me to start wearing a nametag. I didn't wanna. It's been my experience that no good comes from it. People only want to know your name when they're angry and plan to report you to someone who has the power to fire you.

But new security rules required that all staff members — even the funny ones — wear a nametag while onboard ship. I understand the need for tighter security, but with Dennis' words echoing in my ears I couldn't help feeling that I had somehow made the vocational error of which he joked.

Given its uniqueness, I'm a bit proprietary about my name. There are not a lot of Leighanns in the world, and even fewer who spell it the same way I do. The last thing I want is someone leering in the general direction of my left breast and butchering its pronunciation. It's the "gh" that seems to confuse people.

Leighann wasn't even supposed to be my name. My parents had originally planned to name me Rhonda. I'm glad they didn't. I don't look like a Rhonda. But that's the name I give when they ask at Starbucks. When they're busy, they ask your name, scribble it on your cup, and then call you when you're order's ready. Wary New Yorker that I am, this makes me uncomfortable. So to preserve my anonymity, Rhonda has become my Starbucks identity. Thankfully we both love a good caramel macchiato.

But I digress.

Part of my resistance to wearing a nametag is that the successful trajectory of my career should put my name up in lights, not attached to a plastic pin on my shirt. Stand-ups by nature want to stand out, not be tagged and lumped in with the group. We don't play well with others.

I remember damn near weeping in disgust when Brother Philip, my sophomore year Speech teacher, announced that our final grade depended on a group presentation. And I didn't even get to choose who would be in my group. Brother Philip did the honors and I was saddled with slackers all whose sole purpose in life, it seemed, was lowering my GPA. To stave off what I was certain was going to be academic Armageddon I did all the work myself. Yes, I know I missed the whole point of doing a "group" project but my mania earned everyone an "A." You're welcome.

Back out on the high seas, the Big Beefy Men in gleaming white uniforms who work security on the cruise ship seemed unmoved by childhood traumas, and were even less enthused by my artistic sense of self-importance. They gestured vaguely to the vicinity of my left breast and demanded to know the whereabouts of my nametag.

Preferring not to walk the plank I dug it out and pinned it on. The Chief Big Beefy Security Officer said, *"Thank you, Rhonda."* I said, *"You're welcome, Sir."*

From the age of 30, humans gradually begin to shrink in size.
Emotional shrinkage begins at puberty.

What's Wrong With Whoopi?

When I was a kid, my Dad told me that there are people in the world who aspire to mediocrity. I didn't understand what he meant until I grew up and realized that he had sugarcoated it. Not only are there people who do not aspire, but they also don't want you to strive for anything either. For whatever reason, they don't seek to accomplish anything and belittle those who do. I met a couple of folks like this recently after a show; two old men who put me in mind of a Black Statler & Waldorf (*The Muppet Show*).

"Statler" asked me what I felt about Whoopi Goldberg. I sometimes get asked this question because people assume we are both comedians. We are not. Whoopi is a comedic actress. This distinction isn't very important to the general public, but it is to me. While the goal is the same – to entertain – they are different jobs with different skill sets. (Not all singers are musicians. Not all musicians are singers.) That said, I'm a fan of Whoopi's work, and have been since her one-woman show. Hell, I even enjoyed *Jumping Jack Flash*.

I could tell, however, by the way that "Statler" asked the question that he didn't want to hear my opinion as much as he wanted to share his own, so I said, "What do *you* think of Whoopi?"

"I don't like her," he said.

"How come?"

"Why does she have to look like that?"

Like what, comfortable, confident, content? The lack of quotation marks means that's what I thought, not what I said. What did happen was a noticeable arch in my left eyebrow, which said, "What's wrong with the way Whoopi looks?" He said, "All the money she has, why she can't fix herself up?"

Why is it that people who judge others by their appearance are often so very lacking in their own? If fixing oneself up is so simple, why don't they do it? To this lot a woman's professional accomplishments are not nearly as important as how stylish her clothes, how perfect her hair, or how high her heels. I mean really, why pick on Whoopi when Larry King is disintegrating right before our eyes?

Then "Waldorf" said, "What do you think of Oprah?" I of course said, "What do *you* think of her?"

"I don't like her," he said.

I was afraid to ask, but I had to know, "What's wrong with Oprah?"

"She tells all her business," he said. "Why she got to tell it all? She don't know how to keep anything private."

No. No, she doesn't, which would be really problematic if she worked for Homeland Security but she's a talk show host. Salacious stories and tales of woe are valuable currency in our culture. It's almost admirable that Oprah's not asking her guests to reveal any more or less about themselves than she does about herself. "Show me yours and I'll show you mine" seems fair.

Of all the reasons not to like Oprah, I'm not sure that loose lips would have made my top 10. At the end of the day, she's not dishing *my* dirt, and I don't recall ever seeing "Statler" or "Waldorf" on her show.

I should have brushed off their curmudgeonly comments, but I didn't like the direction the conversation was taking. Were there any single and successful Black women whom they did like? Who was next on their haters hit list, Condoleezza Rice (Secretary of State under President George Bush)?

But the human brain is amazing. Sometimes it shuts off or reinterprets experiences that it deems too painful. My brain did me this solid by offering up the possibility that these Black men – either of whom could have been my grandfather – weren't really disparaging successful Black women while talking to a Black woman. No. They . . . just . . . didn't like people famous enough to be known by one name? Maybe they disliked Prince too.

I know it's impossible to please everybody but you'd at least like to have "family" in your corner. But not everybody gets that. Maybe that's why some people aspire to mediocrity, so as to keep peace with the ne'er do wells around them. But to quote another successful sister, Mary J. Blige: "It doesn't matter if you go along with their plan. They'll never be happy because they're not happy with themselves."

I'm not one to go looking for ill will, but I'm actually hoping I make it onto Statler & Waldorf's list. Maybe it'll mean I'm doing something right.

At what age should parents start teaching their kids it's impolite to stare at the only Black woman in the restaurant?

"TOO BAD SHE'S A NIGGER"

I'm no stranger to the word nigger. I apologize not for using it here but for not knowing whether or not it should be capitalized. Is nigger a proper noun? *Strunk & White* doesn't say and my spellcheck has no opinion. It does, however, insist that the word "Geek" be capitalized, which speaks volumes about the folks at Microsoft. I'm also not sure which spelling makes it less offensive: n-i-g-g-e-r, n-i-g-g-a, or n-i-g-g-u-h?

I recently worked with a Caucasian comic who in the space of one minute used the words cunt and nigger. The 99% white audience groaned when he uttered the "c-word." They went dead quiet when he whipped out the "n-word." I've been told that cunt is an offensive word but through an odd confluence of events I never heard the word until after I graduated from college. I have absolutely no personal feelings for or connection to this word other than knowing what it means to other people. Nigger is another story.

In the post-Michael Richards comedy world I thought it was an agreed upon no-no for any white comic to say nigger on-stage if they were performing at anything other than a Klan rally. The overall rule in comedy is you can say anything as long as it's funny, but when the room went silent, the vote was a unanimous, "Nope, not funny." I'll never know if the audience was truly offended, or if their response was colored (pun intended) by the fact that they had just watched and enjoyed my set, and saw me still standing in the room. Maybe they were just worried I had

Al Sharpton on speed dial.

Thankfully the comic wasn't talking about me. I fear if he had I'd be penning this from prison. Do they let you blog from the big house? Oddly enough I have been called a nigger in a comedy club, not by a White comic, but a Black one.

The first time I opened for Paul Mooney I introduced him. He got on-stage and said, "Isn't she smart and funny? Too bad she's a Nigger." (Coming from Paul, it's meant to be capitalized.) That was his opening joke; the joke being that no matter who we are or how successful, we're still judged by the color of our skin. Let the nervous laughter begin.

This happened each time I performed with Paul. I'm betting he says it about every act that opens for him. In case you don't know, his comedy is the epitome of shock and awe. He's that crazy uncle that says the most outrageous things. You laugh at half of it, shake your head at the rest, and pray the secret police don't come for him in the night.

Does it hurt less being called a nigger by one of your own, than by someone of a different ethnicity? I don't know. So far, Paul's the only one to ever call me that within earshot. So I guess what they say is true: racism begins at home. Perhaps the plan was to desensitize me so if it ever happens I'll be able to handle it. I hope the plan fails. I hope I'm never able to handle it.

Truthfully though, I'm not mad with either comic. Comedy is a contact sport. It can be rough and tumble; course and crude. That goes with the territory. Every time we step on-stage and open our mouths somebody is going to be offended. Some comics think it's their duty to be deliberately offensive, but to what end?

I did a show once with a family of tourists in the audience: Two parents and their two junior high school aged kids. I believe a comedy club is an adult entertainment venue and parents bring kids at their own risk. That said, the show's promoter asked the comics to please keep it clean. We all agreed except for one very young comic. Not only was he not clean, his content was purposely over the top sexual, filthy, and unfunny. It was so egregious, that the next comic looked at him from the stage and said, "Was it worth it? What did you prove?"

Like most comics, I despise being told what to do on stage. As a group we zealously guard our freedom of speech and bristle at even well-intentioned censorship. Recently I was doing a return engagement and received an email from a lady who had already seen and enjoyed my show. She wrote:

> *"I am writing to ask you a favor: I don't remember … you … making jokes about gays or lesbians when you were here last time, but I wanted to ask you not to include this type of material in the upcoming show. Or to say that you have been asked to not include this type of "humor"(???). I know that ethnic jokes, etc. are always pretty funny and enjoyed by all, However sexual orientation jokes can be hurtful and I know that a few of our guests will be gay."*

To summarize: nigger jokes good; fag jokes bad.

My first reaction was to go on-stage, read her e-mail aloud, and tell as many gay jokes as I possibly could. That sounds good on paper but I just don't have the tubes. Part of the problem is I'm basically a nice person who doesn't go around intentionally insulting people. As immensely popular as this type of comedy is, it's not my style. Besides, this story would end with me sitting at a bar recounting it to other bitter comics who'd commend me for "fighting the good fight." And I'd be complaining that I don't understand why the booker doesn't return my calls. He must be gay.

Freedom of speech comes with responsibility. I'm not advocating censorship or political correctness, but an awareness of the power of words. Comedy is funny because it makes light of what hurts, but it crosses the line when it seeks to be hurtful. "Sticks and stones will break my bones but names will never hurt me." That's not true. Words can wound. Anybody who's ever been taunted by a school bully knows that. Music industry executives know it or they wouldn't enjoy the spike in sales when recording artists lyrically attack each other in their songs. Stand-up comics should know it since words are our stock and trade.

The sticks and stone adage forces the victims of verbal assault to take the high road, while tacitly giving approval to the attacker. "Go ahead, say whatever you want. You're not 'really' hurting someone as long as you don't hit them." And if the person being verbally accosted retaliates physically we blame them for taking the bait. "What's wrong? Can't you take a joke?"

The implication is that emotional pain is less than physical pain. This is probably why we have a health care system that doesn't include an even remotely adequate mental health care component. You can get over-the-counter meds for aches and pains but healing hearts and minds? Nigger, please. That's what people go to comedy shows for. Hopefully they'll get a comic that can do the job without hurting them even more.

Want Ad

*Full-service communications firm is looking for an Account
Associate for entry-level position. Needs excellent written, oral
and interpersonal communication skills; strong organizational
and prioritization skills to balance multiple projects and
demands in fast-paced environment;
forward-thinker, responsive and creative; self-starter and team
player; proactive and resourceful; high energy and ambitious
motivated with an eager desire to learn.*

*I guess they say they're looking for an "account associate"
because it's not politically correct to say slave.*

COMEDY GROWING PAINS

Many years ago I got a chance to work with one of my favorite political comedians, Barry Crimmins. It was an honor. I had gotten ahold of his comedy tape, *Don't Shoot the Messenger* (you heard me, I said tape) and damn near wore it out. Wore it out I tell you. The pleasure of working with him was compounded by the fact that he was a nice guy who didn't mind talking to a comedy neophyte. We were having a lovely conversation until I innocently asked that if he'd started in comedy clubs, why he didn't play there more now?

And that's when Barry looked at me; really looked at me. And it was as if he was seeing me, and my über naiveté, for the first time. I was young enough in the business to think that the voice, insight, and humor of a comedian of his caliber were exactly what comedy clubs were looking for. He knew it was not.

He got quiet for a minute, gathering his thoughts. He seemed to be trying to find a way to honestly answer my question without crushing my spirit. He patiently explained that comedy clubs were no longer the place where political comedians were grown, encouraged, or nurtured (if indeed they ever were). His style had become more suited to a theater audience. That made sense, since we were in fact, having this conversation backstage at a theater. In short, he had grown and evolved out and away from the comedy clubs.

I didn't understand it fully then, but I think I do now. I was booked to perform at a college recently and was surprised to find that I was a bit apprehensive about it. (I don't really get stage fright anymore. I've learned to channel my nervous energy; pressing it into service and focusing instead on my breathing, awareness of the room, path to the stage, my posture and how I walk, strut to, and take the microphone. I know that my nervous energy – when I do have it – is a gift not to be wasted.) I was apprehensive because I know, for the most part, that I've evolved out of the college market. Strange feeling that, especially since the early part of my career was built almost exclusively on performing at colleges. I spent several years on tour doing comedy shows at schools all across the country.

And then something odd happened. The students started getting younger. It became increasingly difficult for me to choke down a dinner of chicken fingers and cheese sticks in the Rathskeller. "Any chance at a real meal?" I'd ask, hoping for food that came with cloth napkins and metal cutlery. "Oh, sure!" they'd say. "We have a sandwich bar." Yea.

Eventually, my worry became not about having enough material, but about having enough material that a college audience could relate to. I believe that, initially, a comedian builds credibility and trust with an audience by joking about shared experiences. And if you can get the audience laughing about things you have in common, they'll generally then let you take them anywhere. As my life continued to expand beyond college, this became more challenging to do. Not impossible. Just challenging. In short, I had to come to grips with the fact that I came from the Scooby Doo era and the students now hailed from Barney. I had outgrown the market. I can and still do perform at colleges. Why not? The money is good and it keeps me off the pole. But they are clearly no longer the majority of the dates on my calendar. And that's okay. I've replaced it with other things.

Now, when new comics ask me questions I too now attempt to answer honestly without crushing their spirit. There will be plenty of time for that and other people willing and eager to do it. For the newbies who are truly listening, know that if you have the stamina to stick it out, you and your career will change many times. The trick is to be aware of it, grow through it, and thrive beyond it. And don't crush anyone else's spirit as you do.

Self-help books say you should think positive.
I'm positive that mental health shouldn't be do-it-yourself.

WILD AND CRAZY COMIC

I really didn't want to read Steve Martin's book *Born Standing Up*. I've been angry at stand-up for a while now and haven't been in the mood to give it any more of my time and attention. Even the best of relationships have their disappointing moments and unfulfilled expectations. And yes, not counting my parents, stand-up comedy is my longest relationship. I feel that for the amount of time I've invested in this business I should have something tangible to show for it, like a TV show or a Ph.D.

Sometimes I think about quitting comedy, but I don't know where I'd go or what I'd do. I'm ruined for "regular" work. But even if other areas of my career blossom – TV, film, best-selling books — I really can't picture myself leaving stand-up. But Steve Martin did and I have to admit that bothers me. If he could leave it without ever looking back did he really ever love it or just use it? And so what if he did?

I also wasn't keen on reading Steve Martin's book because, despite a few earnest years in college, I'm just not a wild and crazy girl. I've always been more partial to writers than flamboyant performers. Sometimes I wonder if the real reason why Rome burned is because a prop act set himself on fire and it got out of hand. It has taken me a while to learn that physicality can enhance a joke, making it clearer, stronger, better, and more memorable. It's not always just a cheap trick to counteract the effect alcohol has on the audience.

My own shortcomings play a big part of my bias for pure

monology. I came to comedy as a much better writer than a performer. Better is, of course, a relative term. Most comedians, if we're honest, are horrible when we start. Like a hooker trying to quit the business, some nights the goal is just to suck less than you did the night before.

I finally decided to read the book for selfish reasons. I wanted to know if there was something in Steve Martin's stand-up comedy experience that would make mine less painful. And, surprisingly, there was.

It resonated with me when he said, "Comedy death is worse than regular death." That's because you can relive it over and over again until you really die. When he recounted doing so horribly at the Playboy Club that he bailed on the gig, I felt as though I were right there. Although if I had been — given the times — it would have been under a pair of bunny ears.

It was a poignant reminder that comedy shows can be the ultimate blind date. The comic and the audience show up not knowing each other, yet hoping it will be the start of something wonderful. But sometimes it doesn't work out. The chemistry isn't there. Then the happiest part of the evening is the knowledge that you'll never see each other again.

Steve Martin wrote, "Distraction is the enemy of comedy." I've never heard it phrased so perfectly and succinctly. Comedy is so delicate I'm amazed it ever works at all. What do we need besides funny material and courage? Proper sound, lights, and the audience facing the stage are a nice start. What can mess it up? Almost anything: a chatty audience, a ringing cell phone, loud-talking wait staff… A big gaping dance floor between the audience and the comedian? Awesome! There is, of course, no guarantee that a show will go well even if the physical setup is perfect, but as the saying goes: I can do bad all by myself.

I was surprised to learn how meticulous Steven Martin was about his act. Every word, gesture, and nuance meant something. It was precise. This spoke to the perfectionist in me, the comic who writes down everything and arranges her set book categorically with a color-coded table of contents.

I think every comic can nod their head in understanding when Steve Martin talked about what it was like when people met him and expected a performance. "The performance is just that," he said, "a performance and that's on stage." I'd like to put that on a T-shirt. I'm not a misanthrope. I don't mind talking with audience members after a show. If something funny comes up organically in the course of the conversation, that's delightful. But if it doesn't, can't we just be happy with the pleasure of each other's company?

I am ever grateful that he dispelled the deeply believed myth that "one *Tonight Show* appearance can make you famous." In fact Steve Martin's career, though stratospheric, was not meteoric. It was a progression. Each gig built on the one before it. There was a good deal of trial and error, persistence, disappointment, luck, hard work and <gasp> self-doubt.

After reading *Born Standing Up* I understood why he quit stand-up comedy, but I do find myself wondering what an older and wiser Steve Martin would be like on stage today. I guess it doesn't matter if you leave stand-up willingly or have the microphone pried from your cold dead hand. On some level we're all wild and crazy for even having the stones to do stand-up at all.

Rap Music Then: *"Throw your hands in the air,*
and wave 'em like you just don't care!"

Rap Music Now: *"Throw your legs in the air*
and spread 'em like you just don't care!"

"Maya Angelou" Meets "The Jazz Comedian"

There are almost no words to describe what it felt like to watch my comedy idol, Franklyn Ajaye, take the stage one Sunday night at the Laugh Lounge in New York City. I was a fan of his even before I became a stand-up comedian. Some people may remember Franklyn from the movie *Car Wash*, but I recall his comedy album, *Don't Smoke Dope, Fry Your Hair*.

I always recommend his book *Comic Insights* to young comedians. It's a useful compendium of advice coupled with interviews with other stand-up icons like Richard Belzer, Bill Maher, and Ellen DeGeneres discussing the craft of comedy.

While I didn't get to see George Carlin live, I did see Bill Cosby at Radio City Music Hall. He sat down in an easy chair, center stage, and the next two hours flew joyously by. I've had a chance to meet and work with a lot of great comics such as Tommy Davidson, David Allen Grier, Chris Rock, George Wallace, and Kathy Ladman, but Franklyn is different.

When people ask me who my comedy influences are, Franklyn Ajaye's name is said in the same breath with George Carlin and Rita Rudner. If I may be so bold, I feel as though Franklyn and I are cut from the same comedy cloth. He is known as The Jazz Comedian. I've had my peers refer to me as the Maya Angelou of comedy. I'm not exactly sure what that means, but it sounds better than being called the Snookie of comedy.

I was convinced more than ever of our common comedy lineage when I saw Franklyn live. Unassuming in dreadlocks that are now more salt than pepper, dressed in a Bob Marley T-shirt and blue jeans, he was the epitome of smooth and confident. His performance was effortless, unharried, and unhurried. He is not the comedy snack our palates have been accustomed to. He is the full-course meal.

Franklyn began doing stand-up in the 70s. He cites Robert Klein as one of his influences (of course). He's from a generation when comics didn't just tell jokes. They crafted routines. Back then, they got seven minutes on *The Tonight Show*. Seven minutes! Today we get four.

In an all-too-brief set he talked about getting older, the American and Russian economies, being a Columbia law school student, doing undergrad at UCLA . . . all to an audience that had already seen 90 plus minutes of comedy. And yet they sat riveted, hanging on to his every word. (And I'm not just talking about the other comics who crowded into the room to watch a master at work.)

I can't speak for all my peers, but for me Franklyn Ajaye's performance was validating, empowering, and instructive. I saw the elder statesman of "bring-your-brain" comedy. It was inspiring to watch my comedy hero remind me of the type of comedian I want to be when I grow up.

I read a book about anger management.
It said if you're having an argument, stop and ask yourself:
"Would you rather be right or would you rather be happy?"
But what if being right makes you happy?

WHAT BRINGS ME JOY*

*I was interviewed for the book, *A Better Life* by Christopher Johnson and he asked me to write a short blurb about what brings me joy. Here it is:

Having the ability and freedom to follow my dream brings me joy and that dream is being a working, professional stand-up comedian. It has allowed me to do my favorite things in life: traveling, writing, performing, making people laugh, sleeping in, and staying out of the corporate cubicle. Pressed particleboard makes me quite cranky.

I was lucky to have parents who encouraged and supported my dreams. My Mom said, "Do it; so you don't ever have to look back and say, 'I wish I had.'" My Dad said, "Do it. You'll be good at anything that lets you talk… a lot." For me, that narrowed it down to lawyer or stand-up comedian. I chose the latter since I am not a great standardized test taker.

I had a passport before I had a driver's license. Stand-up comedy has allowed me to work all over the world. I've had the thrill of performing in some of the most beautiful theaters. I've also told jokes in a hurricane-ravaged, third world country while standing atop a flatbed truck, illuminated only by car headlights. It isn't always glamorous but it is always interesting.

I've felt the rush of receiving a standing ovation. There's absolutely nothing like it. You can't ask for one. (Well you can but it's really tacky.) A standing ovation is an audience saying, "Thanks for the joy, now let us give some back to you."

I've also been humbled by that audience member who has sought me out after a show to hug me, shake my hand, look me in the eye, and tell me they've just lost their job, a loved one, they've been diagnosed with cancer; and more than anything in the world they needed to laugh and I helped them do that. It's very much like the feeling I got on September 13, 2001, when I walked into a New York comedy club and found people who, in the face of fear and uncertainty, chose to avail themselves of the healing power of laughter. It is no small thing to know that pursuing my joy in life has brought joy to others. Does it get any better than that? I think not.

Stand-up comedy has immersed me in the soup of human diversity. I have met people from many cultures, ethnicities, nationalities, economic backgrounds, and houses (we can't all be from Gryffindor now can we?). And while our differences are way funnier than our similarities, it is the latter that is most important. Tragic farm accidents aside, we've each got 10 fingers, 10 toes, one head, one heart. We are an awesomely talented, yet troubled little species that suffers from taking itself a tad too seriously. Luckily I can help.

When you first start living on your own, one of the most important lessons you learn is that there is no toilet paper fairy. You learn this, of course, at the worst possible time.

What I Wish I Knew My First Year

I received an email from two gentlemen who were teaching a stand-up comedy class to high school students. They asked me for some advice to share with their aspiring young comics. I asked if it was too late to urge them to choose a different career. Something safer, like a fireman; easier like a brain surgeon; or more stable, like a mortgage banker.

Perhaps hoping to head off a bitter rant, the teachers asked a very specific question: "What do you know now that you wish you knew your first year doing stand-up?" I replied:

"I wish I had known that when stand-up became my career, my life would run on a very different schedule from the rest of the world. I work almost exclusively at night and on the weekends. I also travel a great deal. This means I tend to miss a lot of life's important functions: weddings, baby showers, family dinners, picnics, barbeques, and holidays. (Unlike many comics, I do have friends and I actually like my family.) My date night isn't Saturday, it's Monday.

"Even with advance notice I have to choose: go out with my friends and not work, or work and not be with my nearest and dearest. Remember, performing artists are essentially self-employed freelancers. There is no pension plan (other than one you create for yourself), no sick days or vacation days. If you don't work, you don't get paid. This can potentially be problematic if you like eating on a regular basis or having a nice place to live.

"I manage these things as best I can. I am very lucky to have the love and support of my friends and family. I try my best to be there and they try to understand when I'm not. I do not say this to dissuade

anyone from pursuing stand-up as a career. It's just something to keep in mind.

"On a more general note, being a comic is a full-time job encompassing more than just the time spent on stage. At any given moment within the development of our careers we play the role of writer, producer, performer, director, manager, agent, and publicist. It's rewarding work, but it's hard work. Sometimes the easiest and best part is being on stage. If your heart is not truly in it, if you're going into it looking for the 'easy' money, please don't. As with anything you choose to pursue in life, stand-up should be your passion, otherwise you're taking up space in an already over-crowded, competitive, and sometimes heart-breaking industry.

"That said, I enjoy what I do. There is no other art form quite like it. At the end of the day I'm proud to say that I'm a working professional stand-up comedian. It's not running into a burning building, saving lives, or financially ruining them, but I love it."

As soon as I hit "send" I remembered the other thing I wish I'd known my first year in stand-up: that no one will ever take you seriously again. Even in casual conversation they're always waiting for the other funny shoe to drop. When I go to the bank, my regular teller looks at me expectantly. I don't know what to say. "Um... this is a stick-up? No, no, I'm just kidding!"

I could be having a deep dialogue about the real-world moral, ethical, and political implications of *Star Trek's* Prime Directive, and eventually the conversation will turn personal. My palaver partner will wonder what it is I do for a living that allows me to be so sharp and engaging.

They'll ask, "So, what do you do?"

For a split second I always consider lying and saying something cool like "a college professor." But then the next question would be, "Where and what do you teach?" And I just haven't thought the lie out that far. So I tell the truth: "I'm a stand-up comedian."

Almost instantly they are intrigued. How many comics does the average person get to meet? On some level they are also awed. Most people who enjoy stand-up comedy would never have the courage to get on stage and do it themselves. But as impressed as they may be, I can almost always see their opinion of me changing. All my cogent points about quantum theory and man's inhumanity to man are forgotten, and I am relegated to the little box in their brain labeled, at best, entertainer and, at worst, clown.

Alas, every profession has its occupational hazards, and it could be worse. I could have one of those really weird jobs where if you're getting laughs, you're doing something wrong.

ABOUT THE AUTHOR

Leighann Lord is a stand-up comedian, author, and radio/TV co-host of the Emmy-nominated *StarTalk* with Dr. Neil de Grasse Tyson. She has performed for U.S. troops in the Middle East and has appeared on HBO, Lifetime, Comedy Central, and *The View*.

Leighann wrote for the pilot of *The Chris Rock Show,* is a contributor to the *Huffington Post,* and is the author of *Dict Jokes: Alternate Definitions for Words You've Probably Never Heard of But Will Definitely Never Forget,* which was nominated for a Wheatley Award.

A workaholic, control freak, perfectionist, Leighann received her BA degree in Journalism and Creative Writing from Baruch College, City University of New York.

She lives in New York City.

WAIT, THERE'S MORE!

Leighann Lord's Big Book of Book Titles: When You Just Don't Have Time to Read a Whole F**king Book

Leighann Lord's Dict Jokes: Alternate Definitions for Words You've Probably Never Heard of But Will Definitely Never Forget, Volume 1

Leighann Lord's Dict Jokes: Alternate Definitions for Words You've Probably Never Heard of But Will Definitely Never Forget, Volume 2

The Great Spanx Experiment: The Urban Erma's Best Humor Essays of 2011

I Wish Facebook Had a Hate Button: The Urban Erma's Best Humor Essays of 2012

Happy Black Men: The Urban Erma's Best Humor Essays of 2013

Laughing Liberally: Letters to the American Voter (Contributor)

You've been a great audience.
Thank you.
Good night.